kamera
BOOKS

www.kamerabooks.com

James Clarke

MOVIE MOVEMENTS
FILMS THAT CHANGED THE WORLD OF CINEMA

kamera
BOOKS

First published in 2011 by Kamera Books,
an imprint of Oldcastle Books,
PO Box 394, Harpenden, Herts, AL5 1XJ.
www.kamerabooks.com

Copyright © James Clarke 2011
Series Editor: Hannah Patterson

The right of James Clarke to be identified as the author of this work has been
asserted in accordance with the Copyright, Designs and Patents Act 1988.

All rights reserved. No part of this book may be reproduced, stored
in or introduced into a retrieval system, or transmitted, in any form
or by any means (electronic, mechanical, photocopying, recording or
otherwise) without the written permission of the publishers.

Any person who does any unauthorised act in relation to this publication
may be liable to criminal prosecution and civil claims for damages.

A CIP catalogue record for this book is available from the British Library.

ISBN 978-1-84243-305-8

2 4 6 8 10 9 7 5 3 1

Typeset by Elsa Mathern
Printed and bound by JF Print Ltd, Sparkford, Somerset

For Jenny,
who brought colour to a monochrome life.

ACKNOWLEDGEMENTS

Thank you to Hannah Patterson for commissioning this project and to Anne Hudson for her patience and precision. Thanks also to the fine folks in the library at Hereford College of Arts: Jo Lacy, Becky Roberts and Ashley Nunn, and, finally, to Innes Jones, Steve Hanson and Mark Woods.

CONTENTS

INTRODUCTION

Tracking shots are a question of morality. Jean-Luc Godard[1]

One reason to go to the movies is because we seek more poetry, joy and transcendence in our lives. Jim Kitses[2]

As soon as it is formed, the skin of history peels off as film. André Bazin[3]

I don't make the film. I'm only its conscious organiser. Jean-Luc Godard[4]

Just imagine…

In the darkness of a film-museum warehouse in Buenos Aires, in the spring of 2008, a pair of hands lifted the lid from a dusty box. The treasure hunter smiled. This was the discovery they had dreamed of, always believing it might be real. From the box, the hands lifted the can and pushed the dust away from its lid, revealing a tattered and fading label on which was marked the ten-letter word: *Metropolis*.

Granted, perhaps I'm over-dramatising this significant moment in film history and film preservation; but the fact remains: on that spring day in Buenos Aires, a lost treasure was at last recovered and the full picture has now been revealed. The full narrative of a landmark film, and its place in the grand tradition of movie movements, could be seen. Eighty-two years after its original release, *Metropolis* could finally be screened in its complete form, the full span of its human drama playing out against its immense, intricately designed and mesmerising future world. *Metropolis*, like all of the films explored in this book, has, I think, the power to transform the medium, transport the audience and transcend the immediate context of being 'just' a film.

Consider a Renaissance painting. That was the first image I was asked to think about when I enrolled as a student of film at the University of Warwick. Our teacher, VF Perkins (the last time I saw him, in the summer of 1993, I'm happy to recall that he was wearing a Foghorn Leghorn T-shirt), ran a series of still images on screen and encouraged us to think about how they functioned. We were perplexed. We were there to study films – pictures that moved and had sound too. Soon enough, however, we began to get into the flow of thinking that he was hoping we'd find. During the following session, we were asked to select a photograph from a magazine of our choice. Our assignment was to write a short essay about the qualities we perceived in the image, explaining how the image prompted us to respond. Finally, as we edged towards the end of our first term, with VF teaching, we began to think about moving pictures, excavating ideas about, and responses to, the ways in which they beguiled us. The real epiphany, though, came when VF put the austere domestic Japanese drama *Late Spring* (Yasujiro Ozu, 1952) on a level playing field with the playful and ultra-Hollywood movie musical *The Pirate* (Vincente Minnelli, 1948), claiming that both movies offered insights into human experience and did so via an inventive and rigorous filmic style. I guess you could say that we were treasure hunting. Perhaps that's the key activity that we, and the cinema, have in common.

No matter what the form, the genre, the era, the intention, the reception or the source of origin, films send their characters, and, by necessary extension, their audiences, on journeys to unlock ways of seeing themselves and the world. It's a journey that never ends, appealing to both our voyeurism and our narcissism.

We watch films, then, to uncover their secrets and to enjoy and understand their re-imaginings of the world. We also make efforts to work out how the mysterious allure of storytelling functions as it spins its charms, threading them through our daily lives and often delivering a sucker punch to the soul. Often we don't even realise this is happening. We're just grateful for being entertained, whether by the 'seriousness' of a Bergman film or the outright kinetic comedy of a Chuck Jones film.

The movies are about us. You and I. We *are* the movies. I use that word 'movie' sincerely: moving pictures are the form and they move our thoughts and feelings to new places.

Telling stories is an essential part of what it is to be human and the enjoyment in sharing stories is one way of connecting our individual, sometimes enclosed, experience with the wider world. Narratives are one of the primal and powerful ways in which we strive to understand our place and our relationship to our own selves and to others, as we are and as we would like to be. In his creatively empowering book, *The Origin of Stories*, Brian Boyd writes that 'Art becomes compulsive because it arouses pleasure, and it arouses pleasure because, like play, it fine-tunes our systems'[5]

This *Kamera Books* title explores the ways in which a range of key iconic movies from around the world have opened our hearts and minds, fine-tuned our systems (to borrow from the excerpt above), and served to advance, and evolve, the place, impact and possibilities of cinema globally.

In a landmark essay about cinema, the film theorists Jean-Luc Comolli and Paul Narboni indicate that 'every film is political, inasmuch as it is determined by the ideology which produces it'.[6] For Comolli and Narboni, our sense of reality depends on the dominant ideology at work in a given culture. As with so much else, context is all, and movies are as potent in their political resonances as any other perceived work of art. What I'm trying to get at here is that I believe movies matter – and that's why I care about what they can mean to audiences.

The qualities that Jim Kitses suggests a film possesses, as quoted above, are, I think, very true of the films discussed and cited in this book.

Jean Renoir, the film director of titles such as *La Grande Illusion* (1937) and *La bête humaine* (1938), once encouraged fellow filmmaker Bernardo Bertolucci to always leave a door open on his film set. When Bertolucci asked why, Renoir explained that this would allow the unexpected and the spontaneous to weave its way into the essentially predetermined world of film production. Who knew what might pass by, or occur just beyond the world of recreated, re-staged, re-imagined life? Certainly, Renoir's is a good creative lesson and, like many such lessons, serves as a pretty viable life lesson too. What Renoir was getting at underpins many, if not all, of the films explored in this book. I'm okay with being sweepingly sentimental here: the films written about on these pages enrich life and light up our hearts and minds.

Films, then, can be many things: a compass, a comfort, a confounding confection, a challenge, a compulsion to review the world. The American philosopher Stanley Cavell wrote that 'the question of what becomes of objects when they are filmed and screened has only one source of data for its answer namely the appearance and significance of just those objects and people that are in fact to be found in the succession of films, or passages of film, that matter to us.'[7]

Film gives our imaginations the chance to elevate and expand themselves, to open out the range of our sensibilities, and variously transform our everyday experiences and feelings. This remains the great allure of motion pictures, whether a faithful recreation of life in a north-Canadian Eskimo culture or a comically absurd 'animated' allegory of the Cold War.

Motion pictures are emotion pictures, each one couched in the language of a particular moment in time. Films are also intellectual experiences, social experiences, economic experiences, political experiences and spiritual experiences. Just view Carl Theodor Dreyer's film *The Passion of Joan of Arc* (1928) alongside Ingmar Bergman's *The Seventh Seal* (1957) to get a glimmer of that capacity.

To reinforce the point that the more things change the more they stay the same, it's worth relating the following information. In the days of the earliest cinema, as the nineteenth century drew to a close and the twentieth century began, the Mexican newspaper *El Monitor Republica* described the Kinetoscope, as it was called then, in a manner that remains relevant to the current, emerging, digital-cinema age of performance capture and of computer gaming: 'The illusion is complete and the effect marvellous. The images come to life before your eyes and move, walk and dance as if they were flesh and bone... there seems to be a soul in the body of the little figures.'[8]

Consider a quiet scene in a movie about the fury and confusion of war. Two soldiers from opposing armies sit in a window and seek to understand one another and the complex and fragile situation in which they are engulfed. A flower blossoms delicately in the background, expressing as much about the scene as any dialogue could – perhaps more. It's a thoughtful, simple and elegant composition, and this moment at the heart of *La Grande Illusion* is fuelled by what we might think of as an essential human truth: that the greatest revelation of character comes in life's quietest and smallest moments. In so many of the films discussed in this book, those moments are their particular strength, and maybe even their preoccupation. It's in the recreation and re-imagining of these precious moments that we might say film has its most realistic and affecting power.

Film changes over time. It carries ideas and sends opinions racing around the bloodstream of the culture. Film evolves, responding to its environment and moment in time. For sure, film moves, and various movie movements have played their part in the formation of an intricate range of issues that cinema plays out against, reinforcing and challenging prevailing values and sensibilities.

This book is a guide to a number of major films that have memorably affected the ways in which reality is represented and invoked on the cinema screen. Many of the films in this book are what we might think of as examples of the 'art' film. As Richard Dyer notes in an essay about why it's worth taking the time to study and think about the movies: 'Both reviewing and film studies concern themselves with film as art. The notion of art is notoriously loaded – it carries an inextinguishable overtone of value, so that we may say that the term "art" in practice designates art that is approved of.'[9]

We live in a world where cinema has a critical and central place in our cultures and our daily lives. We readily scan an image at speed, constructing values, connections and points of interest in it. The image on the cover of this book potentially sparks a series of powerful responses that remind us of how movies embed themselves in our attempts to understand the sprawl of life. More than TV, more than music, and certainly more than sport, cinema was the power that moved me as a young person and in turn connected me to a wide range of ideas and other enthusiasms. Perhaps this was on account of what Daniel Frampton calls film's capacity to become 'the explanation of our position in the world… focusing, editing, camera movement, sound, framing – all "think" a certain relation to the story being told'.[10]

We're at a point, then, where we can try to work out why cinema fascinates and why it's 'important'. Movies matter not only on account of their artistic merits, but also because of their relationships to the contexts in which they were originally created and the ways in which they have subsequently found a line through time and the passage of history.

In just over a century, film has embraced a rich and diverse range of genres, styles and sensibilities, and now, in this moment of the Internet and channels such as YouTube, the venues for exhibition are changing once more. You no longer have to be able to access a huge, complex filmmaking resource to produce material, and you can now effectively distribute your work from your laptop. The novice director from a small rural town can make their work available for all to see as easily as the most well-promoted and established filmmaker in a sprawling city. Of course, this does not guarantee a sudden new wave of brilliance; but it does provide the opportunity, at least, to get one's work out there.

For the past 20 years, film viewing habits and viewing options have evolved. Perhaps now more than ever we have incredible choice and access to films. Where television would once screen a diverse range of films each week, the tendency now is to look to the range of DVD rental and purchase options available. As such, more and more new titles are being added to the film catalogue and there seems to be a hunger on the part of audiences to know how movies are made and how they make their connections with us. Perhaps the most exciting thing of all is that the study of film is becoming more embedded in compulsory education; in time, we might even begin to take this for granted, just as we currently take the study of literature for granted.

As of this writing, the photographic imperative is beginning to merge with something more painterly in particular forms and aspects of emerging digital cinema. We live in interesting movie-making and movie-watching times. André Bazin, in his work *What Is Cinema?*, distinguished between two kinds of film: those that embodied faith in reality (in the camera recording what actually existed in front of the lens) and those that embodied faith in the image, in the plasticity and infinite capacities for film to be manipulated. What would André have made of *Avatar* (2009)? We might want to cite Soviet montage as a clear example of this.

The films explored in this book are as artful and significant to our imaginative and cultural lives as the finest literature, music and painting. *All* of the movie movements explored here – and it is not a comprehensive or exhaustive list, but one that I hope proves nevertheless a helpful starting point – testify to the enduring fascination and mesmerising appeal of cinema. Roland Barthes wrote that: 'Mass culture is a machine for showing desire. Here is what must interest you, it says, as if it guessed that men are incapable of finding what to desire themselves.'[11] Whatever shape or colour, the movies bear out Barthes's observations.

What, though, is our criteria for a movie movement to be defined as such? What is the narrative that underpins this term – movie movements? A sensible place to start is by identifying that a movement moves. That is to say, it changes over time and typically a movement (in cinema, in literature) is often a short-lived 'reality', a light that burns very brightly but 'extinguishes' relatively quickly. Each of the films written about in this book explores the traditions of a given film form and the ways in which these are subsequently evolved, adapted and challenged by filmmakers and, ultimately, by audiences.

The movies considered in these pages are bound up in, and bound together by, what we might think of as a sense of *modernism* – an idea about western life that has developed since the eighteenth century when the world became more industrialised than it had ever been before, and which was also shaped by the forces of capitalism and an increasingly urban life. Modernism has been usefully defined as a creatively self-conscious format which rejected 'the idea that it is possible to represent the "real" in any straightforward manner. Representation [...] is to be understood as an aesthetic expression or conventionalised construction of the "real"'.[12] Some films revel in these settings, others offer distinct alternatives, but all the films cited somehow celebrate and showcase the power of cinema to transport, mould, manipulate and illuminate. In thinking about these sources of fascination, it's worth bearing in mind that 'the aesthetic dimension of a film never exists apart from how it is conceptualised, how it is socially practised, how it is received; it never exists floating free of historical and cultural particularity'.[13]

The big-picture narrative of movie movements, then, the quality that binds them together, comprises several threads, all of which interweave the formal (the film as a film in and of itself) with the social and ideological (the context). The numerous movements of film history and evolution extend far beyond the reach of this book but are, I think, unified by: a conscious wish on the part of the filmmakers to challenge established understandings about the place and potential of film at a given moment in time; the influence of commercial, technological, industrial and ideological forces; and, perhaps most evidently, a desire to rethink and refresh the ways in which a film can be expressive typically in terms of an acute effort to represent human perception, thinking and feeling.

Cinema has now become firmly anchored in its global context. New and evolving channels of access and cross-cultural contact could either make the world ever more homogenised or could allow for the particulars and specifics that make every culture distinct and fascinating to shine through. We're at a point where a Bollywood movie might abruptly reference a visual-effects flourish from an ultra-Hollywood movie such as *The Matrix* (1999). Similarly, the Bollywood mode might revise and adapt for its home audience a number of very popular Hollywood movies. With digital technology becoming ever more affordable and portable, it means that we can enjoy a wonderful British film like *Seachd: The Inaccessible Pinnacle* (Simon Miller, 2007), resonantly anchored in a specific culture and geography. The realistic audience for this film isn't a blockbuster, multiplex one (though would any filmmaker really shirk this opportunity if given a choice?), but a smaller, more specific one. The economics of digital production and the revenue stream of home video make such a project more viable than ever before.

For the most part, the films explored in this book are readily available, inviting people to experience them who have not already done so. *Movie Movements: Films That Changed the World of Cinema* considers not only enduring 'classics', but other, less well-regarded (perhaps even unexpected and unknown) titles that have been produced as the result of a fusion of a particular place and sense of what cinema can be. This book, then, explores the contexts in which some of the most compelling and expressive films have been produced, from live-action classics such as *Jules et Jim* (François Truffaut, 1962) to the hard-hitting, digitally shot Inuit adventure movie *Atanarjuat: The Fast Runner* (Zacharias Kunuk, 2001).

If you're a reader just setting out to explore the vast terrain of film, there's the hope that this book might be for you. Similarly, if you are studying film (theory and practice; the one informs the other and that's how the wheel turns) as part of a course at a college or university, it might well address a number of key areas that you will be considering and encouraged to think about. It hopes, then, to serve as a first stop, a primer, rather than an uber-detailed exploration of just one or two essential areas of the subject.

This book concisely outlines the key aesthetic and wider contextual issues relating to a number of specific films, and also drops into the mix a range of animated films in the hope that readers will be reminded that animation is filmmaking too.

In the discussion of each film, its concept, conditions of production and eventual reception and influence will come into play. All being well, the book you now hold in your hands will help set you on your way to viewing and reading more widely as you navigate movieland.

Travelling full circle, I'll come back to the insights of VF Perkins. This is an excerpt from his book about the Orson Welles film *The Magnificent Ambersons* (1942). The observation that Perkins makes applies to so many films and is near fundamental, serving almost as a mission statement, an ethos: 'The thrills and rewards of criticism come from trying to rise to achievements we know to be larger than our understanding.'[14]

REALISM

'There are many sides to reality, choose the one that's best for you,'[15] observed playwright Eugene Ionesco, and it's a line that fits neatly with our thinking about the range of storytelling approaches that cinema offers.

Amidst the range of movie movements on offer, and the diverse ways of emphasising meaning and offering a specific viewpoint on, or presentation of, a subject, realism is a key aesthetic form that has functioned as a cornerstone of western expression across literature and the visual arts. It continues to hold a central position, and dominates the mode of popular cinema's expressive approaches. Even the most lavish fantasy, such as the adaptation of Tolkien's *Lord of the Rings* novels, is rendered in a realistic visual style. Historically, 'the impulse towards realism occurred during a prolonged period of social and structural change'[16] when people moved from their rural communities to the cities to find work in the nineteenth century as the Industrial Revolution took hold.

Even if we *only* engaged in drawing up a realism-themed 'list', we could tick off film-specific examples such as Italian neorealism, British kitchen-sink realism and poetic realism. What they all seem to have in common is some notion of, and application of, the idea of realism. Furthermore, their commonalities are bound up in connections ranging far beyond cinema to take in the influences of painting, politics and literature. It might also be wise to hold in mind that realism takes many forms: social realism, neorealism, documentary realism – they all serve as tags to variations on a theme.

One of the landmark thinkers on the subject of cinema, striving to work out the 'DNA' of film, was André Bazin, who was a co-founder of the film journal *Cahiers du cinema*. Bazin's two-volume work *What Is Cinema?* is a touchstone of film writing and includes the following concise and clear-sighted statement, which shows an understanding about so much of what cinema essentially is and the implications of the idea and practice of realism: 'The significance of what the camera discloses is relative to what it leaves hidden.'[17] He observed that filmmaking was about 'the creation of an ideal world in the likeness of the real'.[18]

For Bazin, the example of Soviet montage represented faith in the image, the process of manipulating film to the point of foregrounding its plasticity and illusory power. By contrast, a filmmaker such as Jean Renoir would be regarded as demonstrating a faith in reality, capturing performances in real space and time, in a sense minimising the process of mediation, and striving for a psychological realism. We watch characters laugh and cry and we understand them. Bazin was careful to observe that montage *always* alluded to an event rather than *showing* it or recreating it in that way. Hence, our sense of realism relates to our desire for authenticity and accuracy. What would André Bazin make of the digital-cinema age we currently live in, where image making in the movies has perhaps more in common with painting and illustration than with photography? Certainly, Bazin's interests have been built on and developed, cheered and challenged. Ultimately, for Bazin, understanding film realism was a profound philosophical process, and many of the films discussed here will foreground aspects of the realist sensibility.

Fascinatingly, the film *La Règle du Jeu* was dedicated to Bazin. However, for all of the effort made by thinkers such as Bazin and others (Sarris, Farber, Wilson, Perez, Staiger, Thumim et al), the American philosopher Stanley Cavell contends that film studies is still not given the respect that the medium deserves.

To get a grasp on reality in the movies, it's useful to take a cue from discussions of art and realism in painting from the vantage point of art historian EH Gombrich. He has made a number of useful observations that can be readily applied to cinema and our understanding of how realism in the movies functions. According to Gombrich, we can consider realism as 'the value of uncompromising artistic sincerity as against the deft handling of traditional clichés'.[19] This is an observation that holds true for films such as *Kes* (1969) and *Rome, Open City* (1946).

Defining what is real, then, is a fundamental human experience, and the tradition of cinematic realism is connected to Bazin's efforts to untangle the collective knot of thought on the matter. Importantly, and perhaps now more than ever, it rings true as a distinction.

When we think about cinematic realism it's as both a visual and sonic expression of the reality of things described and shown, and the reality of the inner lives of the characters.

La Règle du Jeu (1939)

Directed by: Jean Renoir
Written by: Jean Renoir
Produced by: Jean Renoir and Carl Koch
Edited by: Marthe Huguet and Marguerite Renoir
Cinematography: Jean Bachelet
Cast: Marcel Dalio (Chesnaye), Nora Gregor (Christine), Jean Renoir (Octave), Roland Toutain (André Jurieu), Paulette Dubost (Lisette)

Synopsis

The film begins in Paris. It is 1939 and thirty-something aviation hero André Jurieu arrives safely from his solo, twenty-three-hour transatlantic flight. The woman André loves is not there to greet him, but his steadfast friend Octave is. Across town, Robert Chesnaye and his wife Christine live the high-life in Paris. Christine is the woman André is in love with and had hoped would be there to give him a hero's welcome. Robert has planned a weekend away at his chateau and amongst the many guests will be his good friends Octave and André. The weekend begins and what unfolds is a cascade of romantic entanglements in which tragedy and comedy interweave. Overseeing the knot of revelations and falsehoods is Octave. Critically, Chesnaye gives a poacher a job as a servant and the servant begins to flirt with the wife of the gamekeeper, Schumacher. André mopes around the country house and finally tells Christine that he loves her and wants to leave with her to start a new life. Chesnaye accepts the news about André and Christine with great civility. The film climaxes with Christine telling Octave that it is he whom she *really* loves. Schumacher subsequently mistakes Christine for his wife, Lisette, and thinks that she and Octave are having an affair. Tragedy ensues as the perils, pleasures and pains of love crystallise.

Concept

Renoir's films have often featured in lists of the greatest films ever made, yet his name will most likely be virtually unknown to many contemporary filmgoers. Today, Renoir's movies would be marketed as 'art house', perhaps implying something obscure about them. However, Renoir's films possess great accessibility and feeling and are steeped not only in a sense of cinema's potential but also the humanistic traditions of literature. The characterisation found in Renoir's films tends to possess a richness and contradiction that we would not be surprised to encounter in 'classic' works of literature such as were written by Jane Austen or Thomas Hardy, and this literary affinity evidences itself very clearly as La Règle du Jeu begins by quoting the French writer Beaumarchais. Throughout, the film also succeeds in evoking something of the comic, criss-crossing, romantic misunderstandings of the play A Midsummer Night's Dream. Like his literary antecedents, Renoir uses the machinery of storytelling to untangle the subtleties and difficulties, triumphs and stupidities of human interaction, exploring the ways in which we connect with, and so often disconnect from, the people to whom we are closest, the ones we love the most. Herein, we can identify a fundamental sense of how Renoir's contribution to the life of realism in cinema works. The broad span of narrative filmmaking had always functioned on a cause and effect pattern, powerfully underpinned by our expectations of a given genre (horror, western, thriller, science fiction, romance, tragedy, comedy), but Renoir focused with a kind of surgical precision on exploring the cause and effect of human choices.

Jean Renoir is synonymous, then, with the idea of humanistic cinema. We might even suggest that he is a cinematic equivalent of writers like Charles Dickens, Willa Cather, George Eliot, Leo Tolstoy and Mark Twain.

Of his sense of cinema, Renoir commented that 'I'm most attracted to the idea of constructing a film from small, complete pieces. The only problem is that this often works against me because of my obsessions, of slightly neglecting the importance of storyline. I'm obsessed with the idea that in reality the story isn't very important'.[20]

Renoir's mode of filmic expression developed at a time when cinema was making a real push towards realism in terms of both describing (re-creating) a specific place and also in terms of giving a realistic presentation of human interaction, from which the film offers what we might consider to be a realistic, and recognisable, and generally agreed upon 'moral' to the story. Given how highly regarded Renoir's films have been over the last 40 years, it is worth noting that, like many other filmmakers, during his lifetime his films were not readily embraced by the majority. We could consider that Renoir's films were largely underestimated, perhaps even misunderstood, upon their original release. It was only in the 1960s and 1970s that Renoir's films began to enjoy a recognition that endures, both for their use of technique and for their understanding of all the qualities that define us as both angels and devils.

Renoir's fascination with the highly accessible form of the Hollywood movie surely informed aspects of his own creative process, rather as it did with another filmmaker, Satyajit Ray, who carried the legacy of Renoir into the 1950s. In the case of both filmmakers, whilst their films may be set in cultures and at moments in time somewhat removed from our own, they are presented in a very accessible way, trading on cinema's ability to keep us entranced, from shot to shot and from sequence to sequence.

Renoir belongs to the French movement of poetic realism and his films became increasingly political and personal as they dramatised issues around religion and socialism. Like Martin Scorsese and Robert De Niro, Steven Spielberg and Richard Dreyfuss, Ingmar Bergman and Liv Ullmann, Alfred Hitchcock and Cary Grant, John Ford and John Wayne, Michael Powell and Roger Livesey, George Lucas and Harrison Ford, to name but a few, Jean Renoir enjoyed a productive collaboration with a key actor, in this case the mighty Jean Gabin. Their work together in *La bête humaine* and *La Grande Illusion*, amongst others, was seen as part of the effort that brought increasing realism to the process of cinema acting. In the book *Movie Acting: The Film Reader*, we are told that 'the film actor must seem to be his character in such a way that all his expressions, gestures and poses point beyond themselves... they must breathe a certain casualness marking them as fragments of an inexhaustible texture'.[21]

Renoir's films have been noted for seizing the opportunity to show cross sections of society in all their separateness and unity. His films aspire to reach the truth of a feeling and explore the dynamic between the individual and their social milieu found in our feelings of confusion, affection, despair and joy.

In his later films, those from the 1950s and 1960s, Renoir explores more openly cinema's capacity to combine emotional realism with a level of artifice. His film *The River* (1961) evidences this. It was filmed in India and, with somewhat perfect synchronicity, involved emerging filmmaker Satyajit Ray, who assisted on the film. Ray went on to direct the film *Pather Panchali* (1955).

Production

From the mid-1930s onwards, there was a prevailing and uneasy global sense that democracy was being palpably threatened by the forces of fascism, and it was in this climate that *La Règle du Jeu* was conceived and produced. If ever proof were needed of cinema's capacity to stand firmly on the side of the angels of our better nature, Renoir's films of this decade provide it. *La Grande Illusion* might yet be the greatest war film ever made, and in *La Règle du Jeu* there's ample evidence of a political, socially concerned heartbeat pounding away.

Text: Drama, Image, Sound

Some have argued that detail rather than believability is what underpins Renoir's films, and that they are weakened as a result. He was a director given to allowing actors to improvise and *La Règle du Jeu* has often been noted for its elegant construction and use of motif and character gesture to carry meaning and resonance.

Bazin wrote of Renoir's staging of action that he 'gives the impression of an almost annoying nonchalance'[22], but perhaps this apparent lack of organisation is a way of reflecting the true rhythms of life and our relationships with one another from moment to moment. As such, the reality of life in its fusion of the tragic and comic, without almost any discernible separation, makes Renoir's work sing with a sense of reality, of honesty. François Truffaut, who began as a film critic and then became a film director, once wrote in a letter to Renoir: 'I have never been able to tell you how much *La Règle du Jeu* helped me to keep going... I will always feel that my life is connected to the film you made.'[23]

Intriguingly, *La Règle du Jeu* dramatises ideas around the realities and illusions we present to one another, and also to ourselves about ourselves. This film is surely one of the great love-story movies and it is certainly infused with a sense of tragedy, albeit often conveyed through comic means. Some of the film's earliest dialogue encapsulates the feeling of the entire film, such as this line spoken by André Jurieu, the lovestruck aviator: 'I'm very unhappy. I've never been so disillusioned.'

As the film moves back and forth, embracing comedy, tragedy and farce, the action is underpinned by a sense that communication is difficult and miscommunication dangerously easy. Furthermore, the movie suggests that, amidst the inevitable difficulties of the heart, there is a need, nevertheless, to find a way of doing the right thing. Robert Chesnaye knows that his wife, Christine, is in love with André, yet he insists on civility in the matter. Early on he states that, 'I'm against barriers. Against walls.' Indeed, it is the gamekeeper, Schumacher, who is truly undone by the lethal tendencies of jealousy and irrationality. His jealousy is his undoing. Throughout the film, events are played out with a precise, free-wheeling quality as characters chase, flee and criss-cross one another, physically and emotionally. For all its more farcical elements, however, this is a tragic story that recognises the inadequacies in all of us and the wider culture. Octave says to Christine, 'It's another sign of the times – everyone lies.' The last image of the film is of shadows moving across a wall. Light is fading from the world.

In terms of visual style, *La Règle du Jeu* employs deep focus, a technique that fits with our own unmediated perception of the physical world around us. It was the product of technological evolutions in lighting and also of photojournalism.[24]

The film was an anti-war statement, amongst other things, about a world running out of control, and the French government banned the film for its allegedly unpatriotic tone. American writer-director Cameron Crowe has said of *La Règle du Jeu*: '(Octave) carries the pain of the movie throughout.'[25] The ensemble device of Renoir's film perhaps informed Crowe's own *Elizabethtown* (2005).

Reception and Legacy

Reflecting many years later on his experience of making the film, Renoir observed that, 'The first showing of *La Règle du Jeu* filled me with misgiving. It is a war film, and yet there is no reference to the war.' He also said that the film wasn't enough of an escape for the audience of the time. However, 'What seemed an insult to society in 1939 has become clear sightedness.'[26] As with all of the films explored in this book, Renoir's movie sought to refresh and reinvigorate what a story could be on film and, perhaps inevitably, this unsettled some audiences who expected cinema to only ever be capable of a few hours of pleasant distraction.

The realist mode is arguably the dominant one in cinema and there are countless titles that illustrate the approach. One that stands tall in film history is the poetic realist film *Pather Panchali*. Of its director, the titan of Japanese cinema Akira Kurosawa once said, 'Not to have seen the cinema of Satyajit Ray means existing in the world without seeing the sun or the moon.'[27]

Determination and a crazy kind of courage have been the marks of many first features that battled to reach cinema screens, and this is certainly true of Ray's movie. In our YouTube age, the era that Ray worked in is already beginning to seem like an ancient time, one when the battle to complete a movie and put it out into the world was often as compelling a tale as that being told on film. More even than a great idea, true moviemaking grit was what carried you through, and no better example of what we would now call the guerrilla-filmmaking spirit exists than that of Satyajit Ray, who dreamt of a filmmaking life whilst working as an illustrator and copywriter in Bengal.

The roots of Ray's adaptation of *Pather Panchali* lie in illustration. Ray illustrated an edition of the novel in 1944 and was compelled to consider it as a movie project. It was shot over a three-year period on weekends and it was only when the Hollywood filmmaker John

Huston – whose accomplishments include *The Maltese Falcon* (1941), *The Treasure of the Sierra Madre* (1948) and *The Dead* (1987) – was visiting India and had the opportunity to view a rough cut of the film that its fortunes changed. Huston advocated that the film would benefit from the financial assistance of the West Bengal government in order to aid its completion. Sure enough, Huston's intervention bore fruit and Ray's film was completed and released and began its journey into the land of the film classic.

Pather Panchali truly inherited the mantle of earlier realist films and helped evolve and entrench the approach in powerful contrast to the artifice synonymous with the Hollywood movie. Ray's film is marked by its use of long takes and deep focus and available lighting. Ray said of his work in 1992 in an interview with *Time* magazine that, 'The most distinctive feature of my films is that they are deeply rooted in Bengal, in Bengali culture, mannerisms and mores. What makes them universal in appeal is that they are about human beings.'[28] This anchoring of story in a specific regional culture characterises countless other realist films. For sure, this realism and regionalism remains a constant in cinema: consider *George Washington* (David Gordon Green, 2000) and *Ratcatcher* (Lynne Ramsay, 2000), and the recent films of British filmmaker Andrea Arnold.

But back to *La Règle du Jeu* and some final comments. The film has been widely written about and is frequently cited as one of cinema's classic titles, a term that immediately invites interrogation. American film critic Roger Ebert has written of the film that 'this magical and elusive work, which always seems to place second behind *Citizen Kane* in polls of great films, is so simple and so labyrinthine, so guileless and so angry, so innocent and so dangerous, that you can't simply watch it, you have to absorb it.'[29] Unlike Kane, though, *La Règle du Jeu* is hardly a 'household' name.

Kes (1969)

Directed by: Ken Loach
Written by: Ken Loach, Tony Garnett and Barry Hines
Produced by: Tony Garnett
Edited by: Roy Watts
Cinematography: Chris Menges
Cast: David Bradley (Billy), Lynne Perrie, Freddie Fletcher, Colin Welland, Brian Glover, Bob Bowes, Robert Naylor

Synopsis

Barnsley, a town in the north of England, in the late 1960s. Billy is a boy who lives with his mother and older brother in fairly stark circumstances. Billy's brother works in the pit and Billy finds school far from engaging. Walking through the woods near the housing estate he lives on, Billy becomes mesmerised by them and duly discovers a kestrel. Billy returns to the woods and learns to let the bird fly and return to him. At school, a number of teachers prove both negative and positive influences as Billy's life becomes increasingly centred on time spent with the kestrel. Tensions at home grow and Billy's relationship with his brother is far from warmhearted. The film culminates in a moment of domestic breakdown.

Concept

It is a truth near universally acknowledged that one of British cinema's several key contributions to our sense of cinema's potential has been its commitment to the realist mode of filmmaking. In turn, this narrative-fiction cinema aesthetic owes a great deal to the British documentary movement of the 1930s, just as we might suggest that a filmmaker such as Jean Renoir had a certain debt to French literature of the nineteenth century. World War Two fuelled the documentary film movement and its fusion with the 'fiction' film. As such, cinema in Britain came to be built around a sense of entertainment and education, or some kind of self-consciously deployed educational remit. This is a subject for a wider discussion than can sufficiently be had here but, to paraphrase film scholar Bill Nichols: are not all films documentary?

Film scholar Andrew Higson writes that, 'The documentary idea constructs a quite different social function for cinema, one which posits cinema as a means of communication, not a medium of entertainment.'[30] Of course, so-called escapist, entertainment movies communicate a particular worldview, too, in their own way. As a side note, *Kes* is worth viewing in tandem with a consideration of the still photos of John Bulmer who had been commissioned to take a series of photos for *The Sunday Times* on the subject of the North in the late 1960s.

By the 1960s, British cinema was exploring the relationship between the individual and the state, and *Kes*, an adaptation of the Barry Hines novel *Kestrel for a Knave*, examines the role of formal education in society and its impact on a young person. Interestingly, a key informing source for Loach's idea of cinema's potential came from eastern European filmmakers, notably those from Czechoslavakia. However, the concept of national cinema is arguably a construction; how it is defined inevitably a contested issue.

Are social realist films more concerned with conveying a message than with the subtleties of cinematic technique? This might well be the case, but doesn't technique itself help to generate meaning? Style is content. We get a film's 'message' *because* it's a film and therefore uses moving images, sound, silence, music and actors' performances to generate a, hopefully, coherent style and beyond that a range of meanings and values. Meaning does not reside only in dialogue and characters but in the staging of a scene, the relationship of characters to décor, the choice to light or not light a subject or object within a shot.

It is useful to be aware of just how powerful an influence the documentary tradition of John Grierson has been on British cinema, and also the influence of the theatre of the 1950s. Another beacon of realist filmmaking is Bill Douglas, whose all-too-infrequently shown films include *My Ain Folk* (1973).

In talking about Ken Loach's films we are considering a run of films that exists just a little beyond the horizon of the mainstream. If mainstream films are about attractive people accomplishing things, to paraphrase a definition offered by screenwriter and director Lawrence Kasdan, then Ken Loach's films are interested in offering an alternative kind of situation. That said, his work remains highly accessible, the settings regionally specific, with a love story typically threading its way through the social realism. It's the rare Loach film that doesn't utilise a love-story template to serve, to some degree, as an emotional anchor for the film: consider *Riff Raff* (1991) and *My Name Is Joe* (1998), to name just two titles. Like the example set by Renoir, Loach's films explore a specific milieu and there is the implicit agreement between filmmaker and audience that what has been recreated and staged has an authentic connection and reference to a tangible reality.

But the primary distinction of Loach's work lies in its political commitment, and it is this feature which is commented upon most frequently. The films (though Loach resists the director-as-author concept) are engaged with the challenges faced by the working class, not just in Britain – though the UK is his focal region – but around the world. He has determinedly not pursued the concept of cinema as a mode of fantasy. Instead, he is engaged in using drama to recreate some sense of a specific real life and has worked repeatedly with Paul Laverty, and others, on screenplays that are based around a highly specific set of well-researched circumstances, against which the rules of the drama game play out. He belongs to the tradition of nineteenth-century writers such as Emile Zola and owes a great deal, of course, to the influence of documentary films and photojournalism, both of which have informed a certain type of cinema's move away from the artifice traditionally found in the medium.

Loach's films often imply criticism of the impact of public institutions on personal lives. Also of interest is Loach's commitment to films that are rooted in particular regions. *Kes* is set in Barnsley, *Sweet Sixteen* (2002) in Glasgow, *The Navigators* (2001) in Sheffield. Perhaps a story can become all the more universal for being rooted in a specific place.

Across all of the films that Loach has directed we can also pick up on the trail of Italian neorealist cinema (location shooting, casts of non-professionals) and the French New Wave (jump cuts, disjointed narratives) to produce a new form typically referred to as the docudrama.

Of his work as a director, Loach has commented that, 'I have enormous respect for writers and I don't subscribe to the auteur theory of filmmaking. When I direct a film, I don't try to be the author. It's self-evident to me that a film is a collaboration, in which, if anyone is the most important contributor, it's the writer.'[31]

Prior to his work on *Kes*, Loach collaborated with producer Tony Garnett for the Wednesday Play strand on BBC TV. This programme is remembered as being politically engaged and, as such, it provided a sound basis for Loach's later work. The television work was bound up in an attempt to create drama fuelled by the impulses of the documentary form. There is, though, a fair argument to be made for documentary being its own kind of fiction, in that it, too, is ultimately a construction, albeit based on a reality that exists before and after filming and editing has been completed.

Production

Kes was the first theatrically released film that Ken Loach directed and it was produced by Tony Garnett. The film's main character, Billy, was played by David Bradley who had never acted before and who was a pupil at the school in which the film was shot. The film was shot entirely on location in Barnsley in south Yorkshire and this very specific, regional impulse enhances the drama and its reality. In casting a number of roles for the film, Loach sourced performers from local clubs.

Text: Drama, Image, Sound

Kes has come to assume an iconic place in modern British cinema and also become something of a shorthand for a generation of British adults when they think not only of British movies but also the experience of being at school. With just two exceptions, Billy's experience of adults is negative: they are dismissive, cynical or tyrannical, both at home and at school. The film dramatises the experience of the disengaged young person and perhaps to some degree set the template for other movies to come. *Kes* concludes with Billy learning that his brother has killed Kes. Billy buries the bird. Does Billy get another kestrel? How does he fare at school? How does he fare in his fractious home? Does he remain in his hometown all his life? Does he go further afield? The end of the film offers no glimmer of an answer to these questions but may have suggested and implied the outcomes throughout its running time.

Billy's disengagement at school is set against his emotional, and perhaps spiritual, recovery, in the time he spends with nature, wandering the landscape and enjoying time with his kestrel.

Kes is typically considered a class-conscious film, but it also stands scrutiny as a film that quietly expresses a nature aesthetic consistent with the idea of nature as a source of solace. Consistent with British cinema's realist impulse, the film is understated but enjoys opportunities for little flourishes in its deployment of an unadorned transparency.

Reception and Legacy

Kes has become an iconic British film and also emblematic of the experience of a generation of Britons who went to school in the late 1960s and early 1970s, and its influence can be seen in more recently produced films such as the marvellous *A Room for Romeo Brass* (1999) and *Ratcatcher* (1998), both of which centre around experiences of childhood. Then, too, there is the aggressive, domestic drama of *Nil By Mouth* (1997). These three titles have been described by Samantha Long in her book *British Social Realism: From Documentary to Brit Grit* as being 'best understood in the context of the entire New Labour project to repackage Britain under the Cool Britannia label after the May 1997 General Election'.[32]

In his review of *Kes* in early 1973, Roger Ebert commented that it was 'one of the best, the warmest, the most moving films of recent years… the film has a heartbreaking humanity'.[33] Derek Malcolm has written that it 'is undoubtedly one of the most remarkable films about education, or the lack of it, ever made'.[34] *Kes* continues to stand as a fundamental reference point of post-World War Two British cinema.

Rome, Open City (1945)

Directed by: Roberto Rossellini
Written by: Sergio Amidei, Roberto Rossellini and Federico Fellini
Produced by: Roberto Rossellini, Giuseppe Amato and Ferruccio De Martino
Edited by: Eraldo Da Roma
Cinematography: Ubaldo Arata
Cast: Francesco Grandjacquet, Marcello Pagliero, Aldo Fabrizi, Maria Michi, Anna Magnani

Synopsis

It is 1944. We see a Nazi contingent hunting for Giorgio Manfredi, a leader of the Resistance in Rome. Thereafter, the film consists of a number of different story strands, all intercut with each other. We are introduced to Pina and her son Marcello. His father is dead and Pina is preparing to wed Francesco, another Resistance fighter. Giorgio comes to Pina's looking for Francesco. In another part of the city, Don Pietro the priest undertakes a mission to collect money being printed in secret to take to the Resistance militia. Marcello and his young friends play amidst the rubble of the city and call each other 'Comrade'. Giorgio and Don Pietro are eventually captured by the Nazis. Pina is killed by a Nazi soldier when she runs after Francesco as the Nazis flush out an apartment block. Giorgio is tortured and Don Pietro put in front of the firing squad as his young charges watch.

Concept

For neorealist director Vittorio De Sica, the underlying impulse of the neorealist movement (though some might want to challenge whether, being really strict, it was a full-blown movement) was that it showed 'reality transposed into the realm of poetry'.[35] This became a tenet that also characterised films such as *Bicycle Thieves* (1948), *Miracolo a Milano* (1951) and *Umberto D* (1952). De Sica's first film was *Rose scarlatte* (*Two Dozen Red Roses*, 1940) and he became a major player in the emerging neorealist mode with its emphasis on location shooting and the use of non-professional actors. His film *Sciuscià* (*Shoeshine*, 1946) was written by Cesare Zavattini, the neorealist theorist. It's also useful to observe here how openly these filmmakers acknowledged the influence and example of filmmakers in France, such as Jean Renoir, Marcel Carné and René Clair. Indeed, neorealism was a term originally used to describe French cinema of the early 1930s, but it seems now to have become synonymous with Italian post-World War Two filmmaking.

Zavattini commented that, 'For the directors who used the neorealist form, the aim was the recreation of moments of truth focused around issues of unemployment, social injustice, impoverished circumstance.'[36] As with Japanese cinema, there was a belief that neorealist cinema had an implicit salvatory function in the culture. Films could be entertainment and escape, serving also as a conduit for reflection and illumination. We could continue to confidently claim that in works as diverse as those of Tony Gatliff, Kieslowski's *The Ten Commandments* and Kiarostami's films we see Zavattini's definition play out.

Generally speaking, the Italian neorealist films reacted against the tradition of bourgeois, 'white telephone' films that pre-dated World War Two, and which had no engagement with what we typically think of as 'real life'. Like any other film movement, Italian neorealism has a context and a tradition that it relates and responds to; one which it potentially rejects and seeks to radically revise. In the long shadow of World War Two, Italian cinema saw, and seized upon, an opportunity to revise, refresh and renew itself. Like British realist approaches, the emphasis was on a form of social realism which would seek to document the real and typically harder aspects of impoverished lives, devoid of comfort and opportunity. This journalistic ambition may be familiar to audiences now but, at the time, it was a surprising aesthetic approach and a welcome one. Of course, what was regarded as 'realistic' 60 years ago may not quite be regarded as such now, in that our sense of realism on screen is ever-changing. Defining neorealism, then, is very much about citing its 'realistic' approach to a subject, its commitment to a sense of social content, 'historical actuality and political commitment'.[37] It's worth noting, too, that one motivating factor in filming on location, which lent such a specific aesthetic to neorealist films, was because Italy's major film studio Cinecittà (where Martin Scorsese would, in 2000, shoot *Gangs of New York*) had been heavily bombed during World War Two.

A key part of this historical actuality was an attention on screen to the passing of real time, so that actions unfolded within a reasonable and accurate timeframe, mimicking 'real life'. Fascinatingly, many of these realist approaches have now comfortably embedded themselves in the Hollywood movie style with which most of us are so familiar, and which we typically consider to be anything but realistic in terms of the neat, tidy and comforting resolutions usually offered. In this regard, the popular film provides its own legitimate and established world view, and we might look to explore it further in terms of how it presents stories concerned with achievements and the pursuit of happiness and other kinds of personal fulfilment. Wish fulfilment seems to be a universal human condition after all.

Production

The screenplay for *Rome, Open City* had been written between September and December 1944 and, famously, the assistant screenwriter on the project was Federico Fellini, who went on to become a major director of the post-neorealist Italian cinema with films such as *La Dolce Vita* (1960), *8½* (1959) and *Satyricon* (1969).

Indeed, it was Fellini who suggested casting Aldo Fabrizi in the role of Don Pietro. Much of the film's power comes from its immediate root in the actual events it recreates and depicts. Some of the film's narrative threads are based on events previously reported, such as the incident in which two priests were arrested and executed by Nazis in 1944.

Rome, Open City was filmed in early 1945, in the immediate aftermath of the war. At the time, German soldiers still occupied northern Italy.

Like many independently produced films, the funding for *Rome, Open City* was fragile and convoluted. Initially, the movie was financed by an Italian countess named Chiara Politi. When the film went over budget, a businessman named Aldo Venturini put the money up and the film was eventually taken to America by a former soldier who, before World War Two, had distributed French films in the US. His name was Rod Geiger and his name appears in the opening credits of the film.

Text: Drama, Image, Sound

François Truffaut made a very compelling observation about the war-film genre when he said that 'the effective war film is often the one in which the action begins *after* the war, when there is nothing but ruins and desolation everywhere: Rossellini's *Germany Year Zero* (1947) and, above all, Alain Resnais' *Nuit et brouillard*, the greatest film ever made.'[38]

Rome, Open City transformed familiar still images of war into moving pictures for the Italian audience, and the intricate interweaving of its various narrative strands lends a real energy and tension to the drama of a number of disparate characters struggling to survive the trauma of war. In his BFI monograph, David Forgacs notes that certain images in the film reference drawings and paintings of anti-fascists being shot by artists such as Ennio Morlotti, Aligi Sassu and Ernesto Treccani, and that these would have been familiar in 1943–4.

Like so many of the most affecting war films, combat is not really the focus of *Rome, Open City*'s narrative. Instead, the concern is with the emotional toll of war on ordinary people. *Rome, Open City* has a melancholy about it, but it is not without a sense of hope, and the film often uses very sentimental music to amplify the feeling of a scene.

Amidst the film's stark presentation and re-creation of the trauma of war, there is a sense of its perceived role as something of a rallying cry for the Italian people as they emerged from the war. Indeed, perhaps the film's 'heartbeat' scene takes place on a stairway where the exhausted Pina and her fiancé, Francesco – so still and placid, almost Christ-like – talk about how to endure the trauma. Francesco quietly says that 'we mustn't be afraid because we're on the just path'.

Enhancing the drama is its real-world setting amidst the bombed-out streets and ruined buildings of Rome. Inevitably, this lends authenticity and an intensified sense of loss and anguish to the personal stories. Whilst the film valorises the anti-fascist movement, and rightly so, *Rome, Open City* suggests that not all of the Nazi soldiers were as monstrous as the Major, who is the film's personification of the brutality and inhumanity of fascism. In the lounge, a drunken Nazi speaks openly about the immorality of their project and the Major tries to silence the Captain as he talks about the futility of the situation. This humanising of the enemy echoes the example of Jean Renoir's *La Grande Illusion*.

In a line that is echoed many years later in Brian De Palma's war film *Casualties of War* (1989), Don Pietro says before dying, 'It's not difficult to die well. The difficult thing is to live right.'

Reception and Legacy

Once Italy began, economically and socially, to restore itself after the Second World War, films that were critical of, and which interrogated, social problems seemed less prescient and popular. This bigger-picture response sits alongside the fact that the key players in the movement (Messrs Rossellini, De Sica and Visconti) had headed into the neorealist sunset in pursuit of new subjects and ways of seeing and showing. By 1949 the Italian government felt that the kinds of specifics that neorealism was exploring were too much about capturing a sense of reality.

No flame of passion and enthusiasm ever really dies out, however; instead, it gets passed along, and so it was that, in India, aspiring filmmaker, Satyajit Ray took the example of neorealism to heart and used its principles as an approach to the stories he was telling. His first film, *Pather Panchali*, is fulsome evidence of this. Certainly, in New York, a young man named Martin Scorsese had found an affinity with neorealism and it went on to be adopted by him in a range of feature films that he directed (*Raging Bull*, *Bringing Out the Dead* and *GoodFellas*), where the ordinary was often rendered in the company of a film style that often touched on the Expressionistic.

Rome, Open City was first shown on 24 September 1945 and Rossellini felt the film could have been more positively received by the press. Nonetheless, it became the most popular Italian movie of that year. Undoubtedly, the film impacted on Spielberg's representation of the Holocaust in his film drama *Schindler's List* (1993).

The film was widely reviewed and has remained a 'classic' that certainly stands as one of the great war films, garnering its effects, like several others in the genre, not from recreations of the battlefield but from dramatising the cost of war on ordinary people at home. Jean-Luc Godard commented that 'all roads lead to *Rome, Open City*'.[39]

The Plague Dogs (1982)

Directed by: Martin Rosen
Written by: Martin Rosen
Produced by: Martin Rosen
Edited by: Richard Harkness
Cast: John Hurt (Snitter), Christopher Benjamin (Rowf), James Bolam (The Tod), Nigel Hawthorne (Dr Boycott), Warren Mitchell (Tyson/The Wag)

Synopsis

The Plague Dogs follows the adventures of two lab dogs, Snitter and Rowf, who escape from a Lake District research centre and are pursued by the authorities who think the dogs have anthrax. The dogs befriend a fox who aids them in their quest for freedom. The story intersperses the dogs' anxious journey to freedom and safety with sequences centred on the laboratory staff intent on hunting the dogs down. Rowf and Snitter eventually reach their destination.

Concept

In her landmark book, *Art in Motion: Animation Aesthetics*, Maureen Furniss observes that animation and realism stand at opposite ends of the spectrum along which all films are positioned. Animation, for all of its commercial popularity at present, is still, for the most part, not taken 'seriously' and yet the evidence often stands to the contrary. One only has to look at websites such as *Cartoonbrew* to recognise the depth and breadth of animation culture that we now have available. A film such as *The Plague Dogs* does, I think, indicate just how serious-minded animated feature films can be. Sure enough, the film won't prompt many smiles but it deploys an authentic film style and tells a dramatic and compelling story that remains anchored in animation's almost synonymous history with anthropomorphised animals. Three other films readily announce themselves as worthy of our attention for the weightiness of their issues and direct engagement with real life: *When the Wind Blows* (1986), *The Mighty River* (Frédéric Back, 1993) and *Waltz With Bashir* (Ari Folman, 2008).

When we think of much British, live-action filmmaking, we readily and rightly think of a specific kind of social realism that was fostered in the mid-twentieth century by the documentary film movement exemplified by titles such as *Night Mail* (1936). This fidelity to a realism driven by an absence, or minimising, of artifice has informed much British cinema and underpinned titles such as *Kes* (1969) and *The Loneliness of the Long Distance Runner* (Karel Reisz, 1962), and, more recently, films such as *The Full Monty* (Peter Cattaneo,1997) and *A Room for Romeo Brass* (Shane Meadows, 1999). These films have a sense of the relationship between the individual and the communal. The impulse to chronicle and document 'real life' using dramatic narratives is very much the language of British realist cinema and *The Plague Dogs* embodies this mode in the form of the animated film. What I am trying to say is that animated films are films too, and deserve the same 'respect' accorded to live action.

Production

In the 1970s, Martin Rosen, the director of *The Plague Dogs*, had directed a very popular animated adaptation of Richard Adams' novel *Watership Down*. *The Plague Dogs* was in production for two years in both London and San Francisco. Interestingly, it was produced at a time when the American animated feature film was in something of a minor crisis, with none of the attempts to revive an essentially classical, 'Disney' style finding much commercial popularity. The animated-feature revival began in 1986 with *An American Tail* (Steven Spielberg's name as executive producer proving a dominant aspect of the film's marketing, rather than the name of its director, Don Bluth, who had already directed *The Secret of NIMH* [1982], which had been one of the decade's earlier commercial failures along with *The Last Unicorn* [Jules Bass, 1983] and *The Black Cauldron* [Ted Berman, 1985]).

The Plague Dogs was budgeted at $5 million and has the same lavish, realist, watercolour backgrounds and attention to detail as *Watership Down* (1978). Neither film is particularly abstract in its visual design. The film was not popular, however, most likely due to the sobriety of its concerns. The elegance of its mimetic animation is hard to deny. That said, through its realistic address, the subject matter assumes powerful immediacy and, in the context of other films explored here, it contrasts significantly with the approach of another animator, Frédéric Back, who is as socially motivated as Martin Rosen in *The Plague Dogs*. The film, then, is stark and political and, in some sense, echoes certain anime concerns. Tellingly, when the film was completed, its proposed distributors were so concerned about the material that they did not go ahead in releasing the film, leaving Rosen to distribute the film himself, which obviously did not improve its commercial prospects.

Text: Drama, Image, Sound

We typically associate realism in film with films that have been based around photographing actual people in actual places (whether the actuality of a designed film set or the actuality of a place that exists). Yet there's a case to be made for animated films also being considered in the context of realism and *The Plague Dogs* is such a film. An anti-vivisectionist story, the film features the same realist commitment as *Watership Down* and, like that film, is an adventure story, telling of a trek undertaken by the characters towards a distinct goal. Like such films as *The Seventh Seal* (Ingmar Bergman, 1957) and *Atanarjuat* (Zacharias Kunuk, 2001), there's an attempt in *The Plague Dogs* to bring perhaps unexpected dramatic qualities to a fairly familiar story setting: soldiers home from war, a man on the run. The viewer is vividly and straightforwardly confronted by the subject of animal experimentation. The film offers stark representations of violence and terror in Sniffer and Rowf's journey to hoped-for freedom. The images at the beginning of the film that establish the animal testing facility emphasise greys, blacks and a cold and sinister quality.

Occasionally the film employs more abstract and metaphorical images, notably during the end sequence, and most evidently in the sequence when a circle of rocks that Sniffer and Rowf are surrounded by transform into wild dogs to mark a shift in the consciousness of the two protagonists: it's time for them to shrug off their genteel, domesticated identities and become primal in order to survive.

Interestingly, *The Plague Dogs*, for all its tonal differences to the more familiar animated feature, has a connection with *Bambi* (David Hand, 1942) in its presentation of the tension between humans and animals. In both films, humans are presented as invasive and violent.

Like *Watership Down*, the realist approach to animation prevails in *The Plague Dogs* and the story is an adaptation of an existing prose text. *The Plague Dogs* aims for the quality of a document, unadorned by too many fanciful moments. Indeed, the starkness of *The Plague Dogs* may well shock a viewer with no frame of reference for animated films beyond the mainstream, and more recent American studio films particularly. *The Plague Dogs* advises caution regarding the possibilities and place of technology, science and military power. Similarly, in both films there are moments when a more impressionistic, poetic sensibility is at work, transforming realistic images to express inner anxieties. This tension between realism and something more abstract is present in all the titles discussed in this chapter.

With its animal-focused, allegorical content, *The Plague Dogs* follows the lead of *Animal Farm* (Joy Batchelor & John Halas, 1954) and, indeed, *Watership Down* in using non-human characters to explore human concerns around tyranny and our responsibilities with regard to science and 'civilisation'. Of course, the use of animals in the service of allegory and critique is as old as *Aesop's Fables*. Dominating an initial viewing of *The Plague Dogs* is the sense that it is unrelentingly bleak. There is nothing playful about this austere film, which seeks explicitly to comment on aspects of the culture, the place of animal research, and the role of the media in our society. The human presence in the story is treated in such a way as to keep the audience detached and critical. We never get to know any of the human characters other than as symbols of larger problems, and the film certainly gains power by using voice-over to create a context for the dogs' plight.

Thankfully, DVD has allowed Martin Rosen's film to find a new audience and to be shown in its full form, with a number of more intense scenes that enhance the drama, and hence the overall meaning of the story, reinstated.

Reception and Legacy

The Plague Dogs was not popular, its serious tone and graphic approach to terror and violence putting the film very clearly in unfamiliar territory for audiences with a clear idea of what animation should be, i.e. a fun, upbeat experience. In the years since, the film has garnered a new audience via DVD and its reputation now seems far more secure. Contemporary reviews of the film included one by Janet Maslin who wrote that, 'Though the film's heroes' gentle, self-pitying bewilderment finally becomes tedious, the film's visual style does not.'[40] In 2010, the film's intensity is more acceptable and, thankfully, the concept of the serious, socially aware animated film is not the anomaly it once was. *Grave of the Fireflies* (Isao Takahata, 1988), *Persepolis* (Vincent Paronnaud & Marjane Satrapi, 2007) and the recently released *The Illusionist* (Sylvain Chomet, 2010) have indicated the possibility for animation to transform reality in order to bring it more clearly into focus.

EXPRESSIONISM

Metropolis (1927)

Directed by: Fritz Lang
Written by: Thea von Harbou
Produced by: Erich Pommer
Cinematography: Karl Freund, Günther Rittau
Cast: Alfred Abel (Joh Fredersen), Gustav Fröhlich (Freder), Brigitte Helm (Maria), Rudolf Klein-Rogge (Rotwang)

Synopsis

It is the year 2000 and the world has become mechanised and ultra urbanised. Humankind, technology and industry have fused together to create the Metropolis which is ruled by the Master. The Master has a son, named Freder, and Freder is sensitive to the lives, or existences, of the workers. Freder rebels against his aristocratic lineage and class to side with the workers. A class war is in the making. A woman named Maria urges the workers with a taste for uprising to bide their time, as a peacemaker will surely present themselves to unite the aristocracy and the workers. Freder becomes this salvation figure. Countering his son's efforts, Freder commissions a robot copy of Maria to be built to further incite dissatisfaction amongst the workers. Sure enough, the mob rise up and destroy the machinery of their underworld existence. A flood ensues and this destroys much of the workers' lives. The mob then burn the robot Maria, believing her to be the source of their tragedy. Concurrently, the real Maria and Freder, as their relationship strengthens, have rescued the workers' children. The scientist Rotwang, who built the robot Maria, chases human Maria and confronts her on a rooftop. Freder arrives just in time to save his imperilled love and Freder's father finally make peace with the workers.

Concept

Expressionism is usefully defined as an aspect of German modern art in the early years of the twentieth century. In turn, the movement is characterised by two distinct, but connected, groups of artists: the *Brucke* (bridge) and the *Blaue Reiter* (Blue Rider) groups. The *Brucke* movement regarded themselves as artists whose mission was to form a bridge to society through their work, and we can look to the work of artists such as Karl Schmidt-Rottluff as encapsulating the spirit of Expressionism. In the context of the *Blaue Reiter* group we can cite Wassily Kandinsky as fundamental. In both variations on the concept of Expressionism we see a commitment to non-naturalist ways of portraying the world. The artist as mediator attempts to portray the world as they experience it internally, often in an intensely emotional way, rather than seeking to copy the objective reality around them. We might contend the relevance of this to a number of other movie movements, and indeed across the arts, but we can locate a similar sensibility in the world of surrealism. This foregrounding of the artist's distinct and particular representation of reality ultimately binds together all of the filmmakers within the context of their own particular movements and filmmaking choices.

As one of the recognised cinema 'classics', the genesis and evolution of *Metropolis* has been documented and charted thoroughly. During its production in 1926, the film generated a wave of ongoing publicity and media coverage in order to build anticipation. So much for the brave new world of Internet movie hype.

Metropolis has since become synonymous with science fiction and, very often, its images of the towering cityscape or of Maria in robot form have been used as emblematic of the entire science-fiction genre. In his monograph, Thomas Elsaesser notes that the film's concept for *Metropolis* synthesises the forms of theatre, literature and art history, and he observes that, 'Generally recognised as the fetish image of all city and cyborg futures, the once dystopian *Metropolis* now speaks of vitality and the body electric, fusing human and machine energy, its sleek figures animated more by high voltage fluorescence than Expressionism's dark demonic urges.'[41] Fritz Lang's films have been described as 'a fluent marriage of philosophical gravitas, visual allure and sophisticated design'[42] and *Metropolis* certainly embodies this spirit, its 'sophisticated design' rhyming with the image *New York*, created as a lithograph by Louis Lozowick in 1925.

After seeing combat in the First World War, during which he lost an eye, Lang convalesced and began scriptwriting. This led in turn to his first work in the German film industry and, in 1917, he began directing for Decla-Bioscop. In addition to *Metropolis*, his films included *Dr Mabuse, der Spieler* (1922), *Destiny* (1921) and *Die Nibelungen* (1924). Lang's work is marked by an overwhelming sense of the pessimism that World War One spawned in Germany, which, in the years following it, had to recalibrate its moral compass.

Production

In 1914, the German film industry was relatively small. The government supported the emerging film business in order to challenge the impact of imported films and to support Germany's propaganda effort. Expressionist art was a large influence on the evolving German cinema and *The Cabinet of Dr Caligari* (1920), produced by Erich Pommer who would go on to produce *Metropolis*, was a watershed moment in fusing the Expressionism already established in theatre, art and literature with cinema. Hermann Warm, the production designer on

Dr Caligari, made an observation about the creative project that runs like a seam through to *Metropolis*: 'The film image must become graphic art.'[43] Other films that have defined our sense of German cinema's engagement with Expressionism have included the titles *Waxworks* (Leo Birinsky & Paul Leni,1924), *Nosferatu* (FW Murnau, 1922) and *Die Nibelungen* (Lang, 1924).

Ultimately, the elaborate graphic style of Expressionism made it an expensive approach to take in film production and, sure enough, the aesthetic began to wane. Furthermore, some of the most creatively vital Expressionist cinema directors went to Hollywood, notably Fritz Lang. Lang went to work in Hollywood in 1937 and made thrillers that were well received. Two key titles were *You Only Live Once* (1937) and *Rancho Notorious* (1952).

In 1923, *Metropolis* began its long and eventful journey to the screen (perhaps furnishing evidence of the fact that films born out of great challenges often turn out the strongest). It was developed by Fritz Lang and his wife Thea von Harbou, who was the highest-ranking writer at the UFA film studio in Berlin. There is also the sense that, in 1924, the project enjoyed a creative shot in the arm in terms of a new understanding of urban space when Lang and his producer Erich Pommer (who had produced *Dr Caligari*) visited the USA. They had travelled to New York for the opening of their film *Siegfried's Death*. Pommer and Lang then travelled on to Los Angeles and met with various major studios and saw first hand the level of industry and investment in place. They even met with DW Griffith who had directed movies such as *Way Down East* (1920) and *Intolerance* (1916).

Like other science-fiction spectaculars that followed, *Metropolis* became synonymous with the immense logistical effort required to build the future world envisioned. The production period (the time spent actually recording images of actors and sets and miniatures) was 310 working days and 60 nights. Filming began on 22 May 1925 and concluded on 30 October 1926. Films such as *The Abyss* (James Cameron, 1989), *Star Wars* (George Lucas, 1977), *Close Encounters of the Third Kind* (Steven Spielberg, 1977), *Fitzcarraldo* (Werner Herzog, 1982), *Apocalypse Now* (Francis Coppola, 1979), *One From the Heart* (Francis Coppola, 1982) and *Titanic* (James Cameron, 1997) have all followed on from the example set by *Metropolis*. The film required the construction of miniature sets of the cityscape, models and inventive make-up design.

Text: Drama, Image, Sound

Thomas Elsaesser has written that, 'In its cultural memory, the film is a sponge, soaking up as much ideological and somatic material as the disaster of the First World War and its political aftermath… had left behind as debris and ferment.'[44]

Metropolis, then, is one of the great examples of the Expressionist film movement, alongside *The Cabinet of Dr Caligari*. Both were films produced in Germany. Hauntingly and painfully, *Metropolis*, in retrospect, contains images that somehow anticipate the trauma of the Holocaust. Its eerie, unsettling anticipation of the Holocaust finds its visuals in images of shaven-headed lines of people walking towards tunnels.

The film has been widely discussed as an indication of how German Expressionism marked a stylistic and ideological break with the construction of Germany's national identity. Alternatively, the film has been read as an example of the escapist qualities of German Expressionism. Then, too, there is the line of thought that suggests that German Expressionism was not sparked by the First World War but already pre-dated it and had other manifestations.

Reception and Legacy

The premiere of *Metropolis* was a massively anticipated occasion that took place on 10 January 1927 at the UFA Palast in Berlin. A full orchestra played the film's musical score live. The film had been intensively hyped, and embedded in the popular culture even before its release, as a science-fiction spectacle. Does that sound familiar as we look back from 2010 and the fresh memory of *Avatar*? Reviews for the film tended towards an expected kind of hyperbole, though reservations about the clarity of the plot were raised. That said, one of the most typical examples of the exuberant reception for the film is found in the following: 'One can sense it: this is the film of all films – the Uber film!'[45]

However, the film's potential and the excitement surrounding it did not convert into commercial success and, for its American release, the US exhibitors demanded that the film be reduced from a running time of two and a half hours to one and three quarter hours. A new German running time was also introduced that was the near equivalent to the American version.

Starting in 1965, and continuing for three decades thereafter, the film underwent a complete restoration. Famously, the film was re-scored in the early 1980s by Giorgio Moroder and the film was re-released in 1984, becoming a cult audience favourite and rebooting the public awareness of the film's accomplishments. In the summer of 2008, new footage from the film was discovered in Argentina at the Museo del Cine. The discovery made newspaper headlines globally.

The film continues to be subject to many different interpretations. Upon its original release, it divided opinion. For many, it was too obscure, too sprawling, and it was ripe for a range of ideological attachments to be pinned to it. Was it Bolshevik? Was it an indicator of Fascism on the rise? Was it a fairytale?

Certainly, *Metropolis* has gone on to influence a range of modern, mainstream, science-fiction films keen to build ideas and new worlds. *Blade Runner* (Ridley Scott, 1982), *Star Wars*, and even Apple's first TV ad in 1984, also directed by Ridley Scott, owe a debt to this massive film, part tech-tale, part fairytale. *Blade Runner*, *Star Wars* and, more recently, the anime movie *Metropolis* have stitched themselves into the wider pop-culture fabric. Like the original Metropolis, they have come to mean many different things to many different people.

The story of the additional *Metropolis* footage, discovered in 2008 and previously presumed lost, was narrated in a piece in the *Guardian* newspaper, dramatically entitled 'The Metropolis Mystery' (written by Karen Naundorf). The piece related how the 'new' material was discovered at the Museo del Cine in the Barracas district of Buenos Aires. Three cans of film were found in this special place and this discovery represented the rescuing of around 25 per cent of the film, thought lost for 80 years. Apparently the film, with the long-missing reels incorporated, had been shown in Buenos Aires in the 1980s, the projectionist always complaining about the long running time! The recovered footage clarifies plot points such as why Rotwang and Fredersen are rivals because of being in love with the same woman. The restored version of the film, arranged in three movements rather like a piece of symphonic music: Prelude, Furioso and Finale, was duly premiered in early 2010 at the Berlin Film Festival.

Martin Kroeber, who was one of the 2010 restoration team, observed at a screening of the film in Hong Kong in spring 2010 that *Metropolis* is not only an Expressionist film but 'a compendium of everything in the air in 1927 Germany. It's a little encyclopedia of 1927 cinema.'[46]

The Passion of Joan of Arc (1927)

Directed by: Carl Theodor Dreyer
Written by: Joseph Delteil and Carl Theodor Dreyer
Produced by: Carl Theodor Dreyer
Edited by: Marguerite Bauge
Cinematography: Rudolph Mate, Goesbula Kottula, Ole Schmidt
Cast: Renée Maria Falconetti (Joan of Arc), Eugene Silvain (Bishop Pierre Cauchin), Maurice Schentz (Nicolas Loyseleur), Michel Simon (Jean Lemaitre)

Synopsis

The plot of *The Passion of Joan of Arc* unfolds over a short period of time and dramatises the trial and subsequent torture of the title character. The first third of the film centres on Joan's trial by a monstrous jury of old clerics. The action then shifts to her prison cell as she prepares for death. She is repeatedly asked to sign a letter in which she recants her actions; eventually she does so and is given her last Holy Communion. She is finally taken out to the public who watch and finally revolt against the authorities as Joan perishes.

Concept

Carl Theodor Dreyer claimed that his overarching creative ambition with his films was the pursuit of 'realised mysticism'.[47] *Joan of Arc* is derived from aspects of the real life of Joan of Arc who was burned at the stake in the year 1431. Joan had heard the voice of God telling her to go and help King Charles fight the English. After a run of intrigues and political dealings, Joan found herself on trial, being interrogated about her life and actions.

Dazzling though we may now consider *Joan of Arc* to be, it was not commercially successful upon its original release and Dreyer never managed to realise his pet project about Jesus Christ. Not surprisingly, perhaps, we can see in *Joan of Arc* the concept of a Christ-like figure being rendered, perhaps as a conceptual try-out for the Christ film.

Production

Dreyer's decision to emphasise the close-up as the key framing size throughout the film angered his crew who had lavished so much energy on the set design and construction. The film's production design was the work of Hermann Warm, the production designer for *The Cabinet of Dr Caligari*. For Joan of Arc, as *Bright Lights Film Journal* describes, Hermann 'based his work... on a combination of medieval woodcuts and the then voguish surrealist movement. This is seen in the otherworldly white architecture that recalls the still, strange world of painters like Delvaux or De Chirico'.[48]

At the time, the film was a mega production with a budget of seven million francs. The film eventually went over budget to nine million francs, the set evidently one of the most expensive aspects of the project.

Text: Drama, Image, Sound

The Passion of Joan of Arc is arguably one of the finest expressions of the power of the close-up ever produced. The visual style of the film is utterly arresting with much of the action over its 80-minute running time playing out in nothing more than close-ups of Joan reacting to those who seek to condemn her. This is a beautifully contained film that explodes with a vision of apocalypse in its final moments.

The film confidently evokes the spirit of the story of Christ. Typically, faces are framed in close-up, the camera angled up from just below chin height, thus rendering the clerics oppressive and inhuman and the beatific Joan delicate and utterly beautiful. Youth is beauty and old age is viewed, with exceptions, as grasping and sinister. A shadow of a window frame falls on the floor of Joan's cell and it is the crucifix. At other times in the film, this same window is included in shot as a makeshift crucifix.

Late in the film, when Joan is taken to the torture chamber, there is a Soviet montage-inspired creation of a sense of dread as Joan sees the machinery of torture.

This film is stark and beautiful. Amidst the trauma and physical and emotional cruelty are occasional moments of grace and kindness and images of freedom and life: the birds flocking over the rooftops, though they also carry doom on their wings (rather like the bird in silhouette against stormy skies in the opening moments of *The Seventh Seal*), and also the shot of the flowers that Joan sees. Contrastingly, the shot of the skull is blatant in its resonance. This silent film is mesmerising, the intertitles barely required to understand what is developing as nineteen-year-old Joan suffers the scrutiny and aggression of her persecutors. The film is propelled by a mounting sense of grief and relentless pain and Falconetti's performance is astonishing: it is almost entirely silent and even registers Joan's anxiety by a sense of intense breathing. As recalled in a *Bright Lights* review of the film online, Dreyer was not a fan of the term avant-garde for his filmmaking, but he did embrace the description 'documentary', again throwing that potentially misused term into further question. The film was based around transcripts of the 1429 trial of Joan, and Dreyer realises this source material as a visually and emotionally claustrophobic drama. This is not historical drama as dazzling or comforting spectacle. This film is beautifully made and hard to watch.

Dreyer's achievements in cinema are considerable, his work fusing the personal and the spiritual and very much embodying the concept of filmmaker as expressive artist. Film history records Dreyer's achievements well and his body of work is regarded as having memorably reinvigorated cinema at the time. Dreyer's great cinematic subject was the dramatisation and visualisation of female suffering. In his landmark book *Transcendental Style*, Paul Schrader (a critic who went on to write and direct feature films) made the point that, 'Like expressionism, transcendental style in Dreyer's films stems from the Kammerspiel and opposes it… The faces in Dreyer's *Passion*, although seemingly documentary, because of their lack of make-up, become their own masks…'[49] Just to round out Schrader's response, the Kammerspiel was a German film movement of the 1920s which had connections and affinities with German Expressionism. The term *kammerspiel* is translated as chamber play, with a focus on realistic character psychology and minimal production design.

Dreyer's other films include *Vampyr* (1931), *Day of Wrath* (1943) and *Ordet* (1955). In a useful overview of Dreyer's work at the

Senses of Cinema website we read the following about *The Passion of Joan of Arc*: 'Dreyer translates the unattainable and resolute piety of Joan the Saint into the accessible language of compassion for the pain and suffering of Joan the human...'[50]

You could claim that the film is a rallying cry for anybody who makes a stand against tyranny and hatred. Certainly, the film distils conflict between state and religion/personal faith, and its conception and realisation expresses this great tension. The image of Joan's flame-cloaked body is terrifying. Dreyer himself commented that 'there must be a harmony between the genuineness of feelings and the genuineness of things.'[51]

Reception and Legacy

Today, Carl Theodor Dreyer is a filmmaker whose name is likely to be considered obscure, familiar to the film specialist rather than the wider audience. That said, his film *Vampyr* has enjoyed a recent re-release. Bergman and Andrei Tarkovsky were also significantly influenced by his work, and Lars von Trier filmed his unproduced *Medea* screenplay in 1988.

Renée Maria Falconetti was a stage star and *The Passion of Joan of Arc* her only film, but the image of her face has become embedded in film history. After *Joan of Arc*, Dreyer wanted to make a film about the early Christians in ancient Rome; but *Joan* was such a commercial failure that it never got financed. *Joan of Arc* was ultimately banned and proved a generally contentious title. How different things are in 2010 with the comprehensive Dreyer resource online. In England, Dreyer's film was damned for being overly violent and intense. The film was re-edited several times, initially being reduced from 82 minutes to 61 minutes, and it was in a Norwegian mental hospital, of all places, that a full negative of the film was discovered.

Reviews of the film have included observations such as this glowing American response: 'You cannot know the history of silent film unless you know the face of Renée Maria Falconetti.'[52] Of Carl Theodor Dreyer, Armond White has written that he was 'the first great film artist to pursue the ineffable in cinema'.[53]

AVANT-GARDE AND ART CINEMA

When we think of the avant-garde, across the arts, we might think of it as varying degrees on a scale bookended by the idea of familiarity at one end and obscurity at the other, with a caffeine-shot of the esoteric along the way. Famously, the film *Persona* commences with an intense assault on the eye and ear as sounds and images cascade across the screen in a collision suggesting violence and mortality. There's an anti-realist quality to this 'prelude' that has much in common with the work of a filmmaker like Stan Brakhage, and throughout Bergman's body of work there is an intense consideration of theme and application of style. *Persona*'s opening is an exemplar of how European cinema of the late 1950s and early 1960s attempted to reconfigure the idea of how film could be used to explore human experience. Bergman's film begins with darkness and then the image of the lamp in a film projector warming up to an intense brightness that momentarily is too harsh to look at. We see the inverted image of an animated film showing a woman bathing in a river; we then see a skeleton, a spider, blood flowing from a dead sheep's neck, and a close-up of a nail being hammered into a hand, which, for many, will carry connotations of Christ's crucifixion. The images, then, are somehow thematically linked but not as such 'explained'. They may appear random but there are relationships between them. There's an openly intellectual quality being woven into a form that even now tends to be limited so very much by a strain of anti-intellectualism; a reluctance to be seen to be thoughtful.

The avant-garde, then, is understood broadly as an artistic mode that seeks to organise strategies to contradict and subvert audience expectation and comfort. It is the sensibility that arguably characterises art cinema in its most intense and undiluted form. We might say that avant-garde cinema is difficult to watch, especially if our viewing experience has been principally shaped by the glories of the popular Hollywood film, which favour psychological realism and, often, hyper-clarity, along with the frequently 'invisible' use of film technique so that we 'forget' we are watching something that has been made. Critically, avant-garde work is often focused around thematic impulses rather than the more standardised genre-driven devices of traditional narrative. The avant-garde has duly influenced the mainstream and certain aspects of mainstream filmic language have, in turn, been appropriated by the avant-garde. In these pages, only the smallest of hints and indications about the expanse and diversity of avant-garde cinema can be offered. Perhaps it's enough to say at this stage that cinema has always enjoyed an avant-garde life. The term avant-garde has tended to be considered eccentric, esoteric, 'non-commercial' and perhaps even indulgent. Whilst labels are good for sales and marketing (and that's what film genre distinctions do so well), beyond that they can create unnecessary limitations.

It's worth making the point that art cinema has always fused the influences of the national and international, and it may be that 'avant-garde' is a term no less productive or limiting than a term such as 'blockbuster'. Thankfully, we live at a time when the mainstream movie has been embraced as an expressive form in its own right, sitting comfortably alongside the non-mainstream. As I have already said in the introduction, I recall being a student and sitting in a class in which our teacher analysed the gaudy and effervescent musical *The Pirate* (Vincente Minnelli, 1948) with the same integrity as the austere and melancholy *Late Spring* (Yasujiro Ozu, 1949). That was a real thunderbolt moment for me, and I have been grateful for it ever since. Indeed, qualities and features of the avant-garde have found footholds in the mainstream sensibility. Witness, for example, films such as *Star Wars* and *The Matrix*, which utilise the impressionistic editing tricks of Soviet montage. Whether short or feature length, live action or animated, avant-garde movies are unified by their resistance to the ultra-neat narrative design and logic of cause and effect that characterises most films. The term avant-garde might best work relative to any other term and creative approach, particularly in terms of the more ideologically and aesthetically conservative mainstream film.

That said, avant-garde and the mainstream can mash together in fascinating ways. Here's one example: once upon a time, Walt Disney and Salvador Dali collaborated on a short animated film entitled *Destino*. It was never completed during its original production period. However, more recently, the Walt Disney Studio has integrated newly drawn elements into the original footage and the finished film was shown at the Museum of Modern Art in New York City. The film is very much a case of Dali's paintings and images brought into motion, showing a man moving through a desert-like expanse marked by Dali's forms and structures: his dreamscape. As such, the film is an unexpected complement to *Un Chien Andalou*, the short film that Dali worked on in the late 1920s.

The avant-garde approach, and specifically the surrealist mode, has been adopted by such well-known filmmakers as David Lynch, the Brothers Quay, Jan Svankmajer, Guy Maddin and Matthew Barney, whose work the *Cremaster Cycle* has been an intricately conceived project exploring sexual and artistic identity. The laws and lore of dream logic, rather than a realistically motivated narrative logic, have a continuing allure. We are arguably at a point now where the avant-garde and the traditional move very fluidly between and across each other. It might sound like a stretch but perhaps even the spatial chaos of an action scene in a mega blockbuster like *Transformers* (Michael Bay, 2007) has more in common with the rush of colour and movement in a 'pure' avant-garde film. Despite its dominance in western cultural expression, realism has been challenged relentlessly.

With the idea and example of the avant-garde film, then, comes a refreshing and arresting commitment to countering the tendency towards a kind of photorealism. The avant-garde mindset that underpins painted art is critical to a certain kind of film, and perhaps one of the most well-known, modern, avant-garde films is the animated feature, *Alice* (Jan Svankmajer, 1987). In contemporary cinema we can also look to the work of Andrew Kotting with his film *Filthy Earth* (2003) and also Guy Maddin. Film scholar David Bordwell has commented that 'realism and authorial expressivity' are the foundation stones of art cinema with its emphasis on the realistic psychology of the characters.[54]

Hence, in a film like *Persona* (Ingmar Bergman, 1966), the sense of place, time and other surface elements may not obey a typical logic, instead appealing to the logic of feeling and deep perception. The opening sequence of the film is widely considered emblematic of this approach. The film begins with darkness and the light of a film projector burning into life. We see the leader of a film with the countdown playing and then we see the range of disparate images already described above. The sequence completes after about three minutes and cuts to the exterior of a building, and then inside to a stark room in which a boy awakes on a bed and looks at the image on a screen of a woman. This sequence is thematically driven rather than by the logic of cause and effect – the film really amplifies the role of the viewer in creating meaning between each shot. As such, there is a connection with the patterning so enjoyed by certain Russian filmmakers in the early twentieth century.

Art cinema is also regarded as the cinema of the ambiguous, and thus may be truer to the experience of being alive than the cinema of certainties that characterises Hollywood. Art cinema, then, makes a fairly apparent effort *not* to simplify life's challenges, doubts and dilemmas. Interestingly, though, art cinema *does* have qualities in common with mainstream movies in the way that it does still bring into play elements of plot and genre. Isn't the shower scene in *Psycho* (Alfred Hitchcock, 1962) somewhat similar to the opening of *Persona* (Ingmar Bergman, 1966) with its rapid-fire editing rhythm and association of images?

The avant-garde is not necessarily easily and neatly categorised, though the films explored here offer useful and accessible routes into a movement that purposefully challenges the storytelling norms and certainly the concept of the movie as 'just' a throwaway diversion. This avant-garde insistence on confronting the accepted way of doing things in terms of making and perceiving has been enduring and widely influential. Other avant-garde films to consider would be the work of filmmakers such as Marcel Duchamp, Maya Deren (*Meshes of the Afternoon*, 1943) and Hans Richter (*Rhythmus '21*, 1921). Richter's work in *Rhythmus '21* anticipates the work of Norman McLaren in certain ways, and so the flow of the movie-making rivers into one another is again reinforced.

The Seventh Seal (1957)

Directed by: Ingmar Bergman
Written by: Ingmar Bergman
Produced by: Allan Ekelund
Edited by: Lennart Waller
Cinematography: Gunnar Fischer
Cast: Max von Sydow (Antonius Block), Gunnar Bjornstrand (Jons), Bengt Ekerot (Death), Nils Poppe (Jof), Bibi Andersson (Mia), Ake Fridell (Plog)

Synopsis

After ten years in the Holy Land, where they have been fighting the Crusades, Antonius Block and his vassal Jons return to the Swedish coast. As they ride towards Block's estate and seek respite from the harshness of the world, they encounter and befriend a performing couple, Jof and Mia, and also pick up an oafish ironmonger named Plog and his wife. Throughout their travels, Antonius is repeatedly called upon to meet with Death and discuss mortality. The film culminates with the burning at the stake of a woman thought to be consorting with the Devil. Antonius makes it home with his new ragtag family.

Concept

The Seventh Seal stands as a landmark title in cinema. It is the movie equivalent of a novel like *Oliver Twist* or a play like *Hamlet*. It has become an immovable classic and, to borrow a phrase from the Italian writer Italo Calvino, not done with saying what it needs to say. A 'classic' such as *The Seventh Seal* continues to feel engaging and relevant in its film style and in terms of the issues that it dramatises around faith and secularism, fear and hope, the spiritual and the material. Certainly, these subjects have found movie-life in a range of titles including *Antichrist* (Lars von Trier, 2009), *The Exorcist* (William Friedkin,1972), *The Last Temptation of Christ* (Martin Scorsese, 1988) and *The Devils* (Ken Russell, 1971).

The Seventh Seal enshrines Ingmar Bergman's early-career dramatisation and visualisation of ideas around God and Godlessness. When people think of 'art cinema' and a certain kind of seriousness of tone and purpose, a Bergman movie might be the kind of title that comes to mind. David Bordwell elaborates on this when he observes that, 'The rise of European art-house *auteurs* in film culture of the 1950s and 1960s put the question of personal style on the agenda, but back then we didn't have many tools for analysing stylistic differences among directors.'[55]

Bergman wrestled avidly with the issues and ideas that fascinated him personally. Cinema was indeed a crucible for personal expression and not solely for entertainment, and Bergman's cinema is a particularly acute rendition of personal cinema.

The Seventh Seal was partly inspired by a one-act play by Bergman entitled Wood Painting, which he wrote to be performed by drama students in Malmo. Other influences were equally specific: Carl Orff's music for Carmina Burana and the Picasso painting of the two acrobats, two jesters and two children. Bergman was also fascinated by the power of religious icons in church, and there are certainly several occasions in the film where the sculpture of the crucified Christ is central to the resonance of a scene. In the book Images: My Life in Film, Bergman wrote that, 'The religious problem is an intellectual one to me; the relationship of my mind to my intuition.'[56] This relatively overt expression of a theme might now feel somewhat dated but the filmmaker's willingness to sincerely investigate a subject is compelling and its influence on the most populist of filmmakers continues to be felt today, with the concept of authorship remaining important to audiences and studios. Hence, we talk about a Steven Spielberg film, a Lars von Trier film, a Pixar film, a Shane Meadows film and so forth.

Production

Like other filmmakers, Bergman gathered around him a stock company of recurring actors, and The Seventh Seal features a number of Bergman regulars, notably Max von Sydow, Bibi Anderssen and Gunnar Bjornstrand. After five drafts of the screenplay had been completed, with Bergman shifting the focus from Jof to the Knight, the film was ready to shoot. Bergman had a budget that allowed for thirty-five days of shooting with post-production (editing, music, etc) following. The film was shot largely on the soundstages at Film City with some location work at Hovs Hallar. This location was the setting for the film's prologue on the beach, for the ending of the film, and for the life-affirming scene on the grass outside the caravan.

Text: Drama, Image, Sound

Ingmar Bergman's work is rich in its extensive and often explicit references to, and re-imaginings of, theatrical and literary influences.

This fusion of the 'new world' of cinema with the 'old world' of theatre has always provided filmmakers with both opportunities and challenges. In an interview in 2002, five years before his death, Bergman, preparing for production on his film *Saraband* (2003), said that: 'When the camera is allowed to play a major role and becomes an end in itself, I get worried.'[57]

A prevailing humanism and austerity were always key to Ingmar Berman's work. Nevertheless, his films shine with immense technical precision. *The Seventh Seal* is an exquisite film demonstrating a fascinating fusion of stark tragedy and comedy, and featuring a number of strikingly arranged tableaux that echo the still images of tapestries and frescoes found throughout. This approach echoes the work of Shakespeare, Greek tragedy and, most close to home, the cinema of Akira Kurosawa whose films include *Stray Dog* (1949), *Seven Samurai* (1957) and *Rhapsody in August* (1992). Like *Seven Samurai*, *The Seventh Seal* puts a man of action, a loner of sorts, into the crucible of a community.

As he struggles to readjust to life after the violence and zealousness of the Crusades, Antonius Block wrestles with questions about the value and place of faith in the twelfth-century world. The film's drama explores the potential dangers of organised religion and its potential to whip the masses into a frenzy. Antonius remains isolated and is, in a sense, a ghost himself. The most otherworldly image of him is towards the end of the film as he prepares to play chess with Death in the forest. A scene midway through the film embodies Bergman's use of style to express theme as Antonius and Death occupy the left and right foreground frame in profile, whilst the central background field is occupied by all the good things central to Antonius's new life: Jof, Mia, Jons and the others sitting on the grass, eating and playing music. There are several instances where Bergman plays with faces in the foreground and background, such as when Antonius, at the front of the frame, prepares to confess as Death hovers in the background, his face only partially revealed. 'I want knowledge, not faith,' Antonius says. Antonius must reconcile his individual turmoil with the communal.

This is a sincere and open-hearted film that dramatises its themes earnestly and finds visuals to express them. A critical scene occurs early on when Antonius confesses to Death that 'emptiness is a mirror turned to my face… I live in a ghost world'. The film sits well alongside Carl Theodor Dreyer's *The Passion of Joan of Arc*. In its one extended comic scene in the forest, the film becomes theatrical and this approach, with characters arranged in tableaux, is employed in the film's sombre climax at the home of Antonius. Do we live for ourselves or for our community? This is the question posed to the ensemble of characters at the end of the film, and by extension to the audience. Jof seems the most benign character and Bergman wrote that Jof and Mia were designed to embody 'the concept of the holiness of the human being'.[58] This is a film, then, that is committed to presenting universally recognisable characters.

Reception and Legacy

In August 2007, Ingmar Bergman died. Globally, obituary writers celebrated his filmmaking achievements. Some commentators, however, were harsher than others in their assessment of his body of work, notably a piece by Jonathan Rosenbaum in the *New York Times*. David Bordwell offered an interesting response to Rosenbaum's criticisms of Bergman, noting that '[Bergman] was even accused of hypocrisy. His spiritual, philosophical films always seemed to depend on a surprising number of couplings, killings, rapes and gorgeous ladies, often naked.'[59] What, though, was the response to *The Seventh Seal* at the time of its release? The film's Stockholm premiere was a great success and Max von Sydow, aged just 27, became a major star holding this position for the next 50 years.

THE ANIMATED FILMS OF NORMAN MCLAREN

Neighbours (1952) and other titles

Directed by: Norman McLaren
Written by: Norman McLaren
Produced by: Norman McLaren
Edited by: Norman McLaren
Cinematography: Wolf Koenig
Cast: Grant Munro (Neighbour on right), Jean Paul Ladouceur (Neighbour on left)

Synopsis

Neighbours is perhaps one of Norman McLaren's most famous pieces of animation wonderwork, although, like Jan Svankmajer, he would typically refer to himself as a filmmaker. At the start, we are shown a neat and tidy garden into which arrive two 'cut-out' suburban houses and also two men dressed very similarly and rather innocuously. The film charts the breakdown in civilised behaviour between the two male neighbours, both of whom are entranced by a beautiful flower growing between their properties. The film becomes genuinely horrific in its climax and nature is shown to endure over human folly.

Concept

If you thought vibrant screensavers were a relatively new thing, you need to immerse yourself in the work and world of Norman McLaren, for he will surely renew your delight in what films can be, what they can do, how they can transport you totally and re-imagine the world. A Cold War allegory and a significant step in the development of pixilation, *Neighbours* – in my experience of screening it for students of film – never fails to amuse, startle, intrigue and finally unsettle. That's a lot of movie magic to pack into a running time of under ten minutes. For McLaren, the film evidently fulfils a mission to be 'socially' relevant. It is also a fantastic piece of filmmaking.

To borrow an idea from André Bazin, McLaren's filmmaking very much puts its faith in film. Yet, like so many animators, McLaren successfully gets to what we might think of as the heart and soul of reality. *Neighbours* is a powerfully clear example of how animation works as a means of exploring explosive and difficult concerns and themes.

McLaren made 59 films within the field of 'experimental animation' and his work reminds us that movies are about the spirit of movement and energy. He reminds us how, in many ways, the adding of dialogue to movies has resulted in a loss in terms of what moving pictures can be and how they can express a vision of the world. McLaren has been dubbed 'the poet of animation'. Certain McLaren movies were made without cameras. Instead, McLaren scratched shapes, forms and figures directly onto the film strip and projected that image. For McLaren, film was not necessarily about representing the world that we observe, but about film as film in its most essential sense. It's almost as if he were hunting out the DNA of film.

McLaren's filmmaking, then, is arguably amongst the most aesthetically pure available, producing images, action and sequences that can *only* exist because of the use of the filmmaking process.

Beginning as a student at the Glasgow School of Fine Arts in 1932, McLaren soon recognised that his interests and abilities would be maximised in moving pictures. He began painting directly onto film, not realising that, elsewhere, animator Len Lye was engaged in the same dynamic frontier busting.

McLaren's work is the kind of output that, I think, reminds you why you started falling in love with cinema in the first place. The diversity and energy of his films gives them a spectacle all their own. McLaren's movies have a powerful quality of reverie about them, unhampered as they are by being shackled to a realist aesthetic. Of his film style, McLaren has said: 'Handmade cinema is like watching thought, if thought could be seen.'[60]

Another notable McLaren short is *Lines: Horizontal* (1962) in which the filmmaker worked with Evelyn Lambart to illustrate Pete Seeger's wistful music. The film explores the dynamic relationship between sound and image, with the music quickening and the lines multiplying with dreamy precision. McLaren's movies must be a mathematician's delight. Indeed, Chuck Jones, the directing ace of the *Road Runner* animated shorts, echoes McLaren with his film *The Dot and the Line* (1965).

McLaren's piece *Synchromy* (1971) is a dazzling, free-association dream of squares and rectangles in increasing combinations and arrangements of colour. McLaren also provided the music and at times you are reminded of the culminating sequence of *Close Encounters of the Third Kind* (Steven Spielberg, 1977). In the early 1980s, McLaren used the optical printer to create certain effects and impressions capturing the beauty of movement. The 21-minute-long dance piece *Narcissus* (1983) was a balletic representation of the ancient tale of a man falling in love with his own reflection. Set against a black background, a delicate, golden rim-light lends the dancers further grace and immortality. The film arcs to a new place when McLaren, using the optical printer, duplicates, multiplies and overlays his dancing figures, causing us to delight in what it is about cinema that we find so alluring. In his extensive range of writings, Paul Wells has observed that the animated film 'essentially offers an alternative vocabulary to the filmmaker by which alternative perspectives and levels of address are possible'.[61]

McLaren's movies have won over 200 international awards and *Neighbours* won the Academy Award in 1952 for Best Animated Short.

Reception and Legacy

McLaren's influence is certainly tangible in terms of graphic design and 'avant-garde' rather than 'mainstream' animation. That said, there is a welcome tip of the hat to his work in the Pixar movie *Ratatouille* (2007) as Remy enthusiastically describes flavours. The filmmaker George Lucas has also referenced McLaren's influence on his sense of what cinema can be, going in a direction that doesn't favour cinema based on characters talking to each other. However, whilst McLaren's films may be formally surprising, in our early-twenty-first-century fascination with fusions between photographed images and the capacity to 'paint' films that we now have, McLaren's work may become all the more inspiring. Of the ideas the filmmaker explored it has been noted that, 'Thematically, McLaren's work sets itself apart through its humanism.'[62]

THE FILMS OF STAN BRAKHAGE

Dog Star Man (1964), *Mothlight* (1963) and other titles

Directed by: Stan Brakhage
Written by: Stan Brakhage
Produced by: Stan Brakhage
Edited by: Stan Brakhage
Cinematography: Stan Brakhage

Synopsis

Confoundingly, or thrillingly, depending on your sense of what cinema can be, *Mothlight* has no story as such; no apparent cause and effect. Comprising a series of parts and a Prelude, the film communicates the musical quality that film can have in terms of refrains of image and sequences, and dynamic changes of rhythm and tone. The Prelude consists of a range of images of the natural world, notably a repeating image of the sun's solar flares. We also see 'distorted' images of human figures. The film has a cosmic quality to it and is refreshingly anti-representational in terms of an easy kind of realism.

Concept

Stan Brakhage made over 400 films ranging from nine seconds in duration to four hours. He created lots of psychodramas centred around the home, including titles such as *Desistfilm* (1954). Brakhage then progressed to creating home movies, such as *Window Water Baby Moving* (1962). With one of his most well-known titles, *Mothlight*, he challenged the purported realism of film by taking a dead moth, which had been pulled apart and the parts affixed to a strip of film, and projecting it. The visual effect is quite arresting as the screen flashes with marks and slashes and bursts of energy. The pacing of a scene such as the Death Star attack in *Star Wars* (George Lucas, 1977) owes more to a filmmaker like Brakhage than the traditions of Hollywood adventure movies. In the late part of his career, Brakhage engaged with scratching and painting directly onto film.

In the book *Animation Unlimited*, Brakhage's films are usefully described as being 'linked by the exploration of a common theme: the concept of vision and the act of perception. Brakhage wanted his viewers to be touched in the 'very flesh of our eyes', and his work is dedicated to exploring the furthest possibilities of filmmaking in this context'.[63] You could say that Brakhage was all about recreating that feeling we all know, which lies somewhere between being awake and asleep. For Brakhage, representing the world in a more conventional and familiar form was not his interest. Instead, he was more interested and excited by indicating what the deeper process of seeing the world involved. As others have observed and discussed in great detail, he was investigating ways of expressing the neural processes of humans when they look at the world.

Production

In discussing Brakhage and production processes it may be more useful to give an indication of, and insight into, the broader approach he took across his diverse body of work. Brakhage's filmmaking was singularly anti-conventional and it's worth keeping in mind that, as an emerging filmmaker, he was in the company of Maya Deren, Jonas and Adolfas Mekas and Robert Duncan.

Text: Drama, Image, Sound

Brakhage's films are not invested in the conventional, traditional form of cinema based around representational illusions. Instead, the films are very much about the act of seeing, or looking, of the neurological process of viewing the world. Regarded as his magnum opus, *Dog Star Man* (1964) is an ecstatic, mesmerising, arresting, 75-minute immersion in the sun, the stars, the earth. A fascinating visual poem, the film is a silent piece that cascades with solar flares, bursts of colour, artificial light and vibrant scratches across the film. It is as far from a linear narrative as you could get and, as such, is very liberating. Maybe this is the most real kind of film you could find. Made over a period of three years, *Dog Star Man* has not dated and its fractured form and dazzling range of textures feels very contemporary.

Because it is a silent film, there is nothing to distract from the images, and there is something of Walt Whitman's exultant poetry to Brakhage's movie rhymes and patterns. The film is broken into a Prelude and four subsequent parts and visualises ideas of family and humans against the immensity of nature. The film is elemental, with the images and structure as expansive as the skies and landscapes that unfold. Through it all, an apocalyptic sheen prevails.

Dog Star Man is a very American film, with Brakhage depicting himself at different times as a woodsman and attempting to climb a mountain. The need to conquer the landscape and the natural world as a way of defining oneself is an especially American compulsion and *Dog Star Man* is a hymn to the overwhelming power of natural forces. Brakhage produced the film in a longer, four-hour iteration entitled *The Art of Vision*.

Throughout his career, Brakhage produced a wealth of short film pieces. A leading figure on the American avant-garde scene, he has had his work collected at numerous museums and universities worldwide, including the Museum of Modern Art in New York. He died in March 2003 in Victoria, British Columbia. Brakhage's films are usefully understood as a new way of seeing the world and the familiar. Brakhage wrote that 'I suggest that there is a pursuit of knowledge, foreign to language, founded upon visual communication'.[64]

Reception and Legacy

Brakhage's films arguably enjoy a higher profile in the world of fine-art filmmaking than in more traditionally orientated film appreciation. What's interesting, though, is how Brakhage's films – and, indeed, those of Norman McLaren – connect so readily to the kind of filmmaking we see in today's world of TV commercials and music videos. Brakhage's work defies convention and there have been thoroughgoing efforts to understand it and put it into a context. Here's a typical example of how Brakhage's work has been described and valued: 'His work consisted of exploring, inventing and revealing other frequencies of possible imagery. From simple abstraction to the visual critique of familiar imagery, Brakhage enlarged the frame of cinematic figurativity like no other artist has ever done.'[65]

THE FILMS OF FRÉDÉRIC BACK

The Man Who Planted Trees (1987)
and *The Mighty River* (1993)

Directed by: Frédéric Back
Written by: Jean Giono
Produced by: Frédéric Back and Hubert Tison
Edited by: Norbert Pickering
Cinematography: Claude Lapierre and Jean Robillard
Cast: Donald Sutherland (Narrator)

Synopsis

The Man Who Planted Trees is a 30-minute piece of hand-drawn animation accompanied by a lyrical narration. We watch as a man arrives in a desolate town and begins planting trees. The story is set at the beginning of the twentieth century and unfolds over several decades, almost the entire span of his life, taking in the changing seasons and the thunderous echoes of war in the modern, industrialised world beyond. People come to visit the man's tree-filled valley, not realising that it was he who planted the seeds from which the forest has grown. People revel in the forest's beauty. The film celebrates the endurance of nature and also the need for hope.

Concept

Frédéric Back's films are amongst the most beautiful ever made, animated or not. Back worked in Canadian TV as a producer of visual effects and graphic elements for programming. Over time, however, he became interested in producing his own films.

There's a tradition, as old as cinema itself, of taking what's known, real and agreed on and then bending, reshaping, transforming and re-imagining it. Back's films gracefully demonstrate how to copy reality and then, ever so slightly, abstract it to get at a larger, more important truth than just the facts of surface detail. This is one of the most vivid pleasures of animated films in general, and Back uses this quality to remind us how we can minimise harm to our environment. His films are poetic and metaphorical and there is a willingness to teach and educate. These animated movies are a long way from the productions of Disney, Aardman and the Ghibli animation studio in Japan. However, Hayao Miyazaki has testified to the influence of Back's relatively small number of animated films, whose quiet power, joyfulness and seriousness of purpose can be readily identified in Miyazaki's productions.

Of his work, Back has said, 'You don't count money or time or anything else when you make a film. Animation is a *folie amoureuse*, something that comes from your heart.'[66]

Production

Frédéric Back worked on his animated films in collaboration with Canadian producer Hubert Tison at Radio Canada. The funding and resource provision for their collaborations was quite different to the more profit-centred work of other animation producers at the time. In his films, Back very openly addressed social issues and now, more than ever, they have a special relevance in this age of burgeoning environmental concern.

Text: Drama, Image, Sound

Frédéric Back's beautiful films have the quality of picture-book illustrations shimmering across the screen. Hand drawn and delicate, they are amongst the most visually distinct of all the films written about here. There's something of Marc Chagall's paintings to Back's work and the influence of Impressionist painters shines through.

The landscapes and images of *The Man Who Planted Trees* are fluidly presented and the film reinforces the sense of connectedness that exists between all living things. The film tells the story of a shepherd who quietly commits himself to planting seeds that will eventually become trees on a previously barren landscape.

We may want to describe Back's work as avant-garde but this is not to suggest the films are difficult to watch or obscure in their content or treatment of subject. Instead, they are majestic, quiet, resonant and compassionate. *The Man Who Planted Trees* is amplified in its resonance by an accompanying narrated voice-over, which gives us much content that the images alone cannot offer. As such, there is a dynamic interplay between sound and image; this is the best kind of filmmaking.

The film's visual elements, from the first frame, emphatically represent the beauty and immensity of nature with an image of the sun in the sky. On the music track we hear the sound of tremulous strings shimmering in concert with the drawings. The sequence continues, establishing a sense of the elements against which we eventually catch sight of a moving figure amidst a barren landscape. The film's fluid, ever-shifting and metamorphosing land and skyscapes underpin the personal drama of a man seeking to cultivate a garden in this harsh terrain. Fascinatingly, in Back's follow-up film, *The Mighty River*, the through line is less about one person's challenge; instead, we are presented with aspects of the larger historical, social and scientific tapestry.

The Man Who Planted Trees celebrates the pursuit of a dream, as well as the importance of compassion and stewardship vis-à-vis our natural world, and, by extension, each other. It's a film about caring, and the images get to the essence of this massive and ancient concern. 'Being with this man brought a great sense of peace,' explains the narrator, in a sense encapsulating the world view of the film in one plainly spoken statement. The images of the film move in a serene manner and the blues, greens and yellows might evoke in viewers the paintings of Samuel Palmer and Vincent Van Gogh and a sense of the spiritual. Indeed, a similar pattern of work can be seen in the work of animator Aleksandr Petrov in titles such as *The Old Man and the Sea* (1999).

Back's 'sequel' to *The Man Who Planted Trees* was *The Mighty River*, which sits near perfectly alongside its predecessor, forming a rich and powerful diptych. Made with the same visual style as *The Man Who Planted Trees*, the film again moves fluidly across time and space and uses voice-over to add a stream of information about history and specific cultural experience. Of his visual approach, Back has commented that it is 'very realistic, especially in [*The Man Who Planted Trees*], because I want to create dreamlike images that are close to reality'.[67]

The Mighty River is concerned both with history and also the importance of developing a sense of care and stewardship as regards the future. It's hard to think of a film that could connect with more quiet force than this to our current global concern about the future of humanity on Earth. The film traces the history of Canada's Saint Lawrence River from its creation through to the modern era. The film's clearest consideration is the distinction between the First People's life around the river and the ways in which European settlers used the river only as an exploitable resource. An image of a rock transforming into the profile of a native tribesperson reinforces the concept of unity between the ancient culture and the natural world. This film, then, is explicitly concerned with, and immensely critical of, human insensitivity to the natural world, talking as it does about 'an insatiable Europe'. The 'First People' are described as regarding the animals as 'their brothers'. Frédéric Back has said that with *The Mighty River* he wanted to communicate the 'vertigo of ignorance'.[68] This reverie of nature has found an echo in a dazzling music video called 'Wanderlust' by the singer Bjork.

The animated films of Frédéric Back celebrate nature and honour its fragility and strength. These films show how we can understand our natural world and share in the care of it. In its capacity to represent the wonders and difficulties of being alive, cinema invests audiences with a profound and immediate sense of their connection to the wilderness.

In all of the films discussed in this book, the relationship between spoken word and image is, of course, a key concern. The short-film form (often with a running time of around 15 minutes, and no longer than 60), because of its need to communicate with brevity, often finds a very dynamic interplay of image and sound, layering and interweaving these elements with a certain kind of density and thoughtfulness. We might even say with some confidence that a short film can often be a more exciting cinematic prospect than a feature.

Reception and Legacy

Like *The Man Who Planted Trees*, *The Mighty River* was screened internationally at film festivals and on television and was the recipient of countless awards. Both films represent a summation of Back's work as illustrator, animator and environmentally conscious citizen. Back worked with coloured pencils mixed with turpentine and applied to frosted cels to create the shimmering, fluid, dreamy images of both films. Both were award winners. Perhaps there is a chance that, in our current, acutely eco-conscious climate, Back's films will find new and especially powerful currency. Writing about his films, Paul Wells has observed that Back's work is amongst 'the world's best animation'.[69]

SURREALISM

In her book *Surrealism and the Visual Arts*, Kim Grant offers a useful starting point when defining Surrealism as follows: 'The Surrealists were convinced the insane were unhampered by conventional reality and expectation and that their products were liberated productions of the unconscious...'[70]

Surrealism has its roots in France, where it emerged during the mid-1920s. Surrealist films are amongst the most distinctive and playful, being so invested in transforming the 'ordinary' and familiar and defying the logic of realist-based storytelling. The impact of Surrealist cinema is considerable and in our contemporary filmscape we can cite the work of Terry Gilliam, Tim Burton, Hayao Miyazaki, the Brothers Quay and Jan Svankmajer as filmmakers who have put the surrealist mode into often very accessible formats. What is interesting about this list is that animation is the common denominator.

Indeed, the work of the Brothers Quay underscores the neat fit and potential in allying animation with a sense of the surreal. Their surreal, challenging visions have energised animation for almost 30 years. Born in Philadelphia in 1947, the twin brothers, Stephen and Timothy Quay, attended the Royal College of Art in the 1960s. At the RCA, the brothers formed a partnership with Keith Griffiths who has produced much of their work since the 1980s. Significantly influenced by the films of Jan Svankmajer and Ladislaw Starewicz, the Brothers Quay also delight in animation's capacity for expressing the freaky unconscious. Classical, normal narrative forms appear to interest them little and animation's free-associating temperament is well suited to the Quays' visual sense and their revelling in films that go as far as possible from anything that could be considered realistic. Their films are like very playful horror movies, and artifice and intimations of menace and uncertainty prevail throughout. Indeed, their films are somewhat hard to predict in terms of the outcome. How things are happening and being shown is very much foregrounded in these films. Initially, the brothers worked in the short-film format but have, more recently, moved into feature-length projects, and their reputation for the startling remains assured.

The Unnameable Little Broom (1985) is adapted from *The Epic of Gilgamesh*, the ancient Babylonian myth, and the story centres on a Punch-like character who rides around on a bike. With no dialogue and an insistent music score the film feels more like a compelling contraption than a short film. In *The Cabinet of Jan Svankmajer* (1984) there's an evident playfulness at work as the film honours both the eponymous Czech animator and references Robert Wiene's 1919 German Expressionist film *The Cabinet of Dr Caligari*. A sense of violence pervades the dream logic. Their longer short film *The Street of Crocodiles* (1986) is widely regarded as the Quay Brothers' masterpiece. Based on a story by Bruno Schulz, and originally entitled *Cinnamon Shops*, it is set around a district of Prague where a man is transported to a subterranean world of shadow, instability and the grotesque. Reality slips and slides furiously in the film. More recently, they have branched out into working with actors in the film *Institute Benjamenta* (1995), starring Mark Rylance and Alice Krige. This is a stunning fusion of live action and animation in which a man named Jakob goes to be trained as a servant and finds himself in a shadowy, fairytale-inspired world of shadows.

Key film titles of the Surrealist movement include *The Seashell and the Clergyman* (1927), *The Blood of a Poet* (1927) and *L'Age d'or* (1930). In the introduction to a printed version of the screenplay of *Un Chien Andalou* we read that 'their textual differences apart, Surrealist films share a range of common interests which are partly to do with the reality to which they refer, and partly with their vision of the cinema itself. They prefer to locate the real beyond the surface of immediate visibility, in hidden or repressed dimensions of the society and the psyche.'[71]

Certainly, the interest and beauty of Surrealism finds its contemporary mainstream expression in Terry Gilliam's work, as his most recent film, *The Imaginarium of Dr Parnassus* (2009), attests. Surrealism informs fantasy cinema. In his book *Fantasy Cinema: Impossible Worlds on Screen*, David Butler writes that 'the prevailing perception of fantasy, whether cinematic or literary, as being "mere" escapism without any meaningful content or social function'[72] has been insufficiently explored and understood.

Poetry and painting have always been streams of influence for for Surrealist filmmakers and, as such, there is something logical and fascinating about the collaboration that developed between Salvador Dali and Walt Disney with their short-lived project *Destino*, which was recently completed and screened at New York's Museum of Modern Art. Continuing to evolve the tradition has been the work of filmmaker (don't dare call him an animator!) Jan Svankmajer, who explores the capacities of dream logic to create an arresting fusion of unsettling images rooted in both animation and live action.

Svankmajer's films possess a visceral intensity, occupying a realm where horror and humour meet. Inspired by Fellini, Méliès and eastern-European traditions of puppetry, Svankmajer formally and thematically subverts expectations of what animation can be and, like Disney, he is fascinated by the fairytale form, although he treats it in a very different way. Svankmajer began his creative working life in theatre and was powerfully influenced by the Czech Surrealist Group. In the early 1960s, he shifted into filmmaking with his first short film, *The Last Trick* (1964). Between 1973 and 1980, the Communist regime deemed Svankmajer's work subversive and he produced no films. In 1983, his fortunes revived when his *Dimensions of Dialogue* won the Grand Prize at France's highly regarded, long-running Annecy Animation Festival. Since then, Svankmajer's reputation has gone from strength to strength, though his work continues to find only a limited audience through art-house screenings and DVDs. Svankmajer's key film arguably remains *Alice*, a sinister spin on Lewis Carroll's novel, and the director's second dip into the well of Lewis Carroll, having also adapted *Jabberwocky* in 1971. For the director, Carroll's infantile scenarios proved compelling. Since the breakthrough success of *Alice* (1988), Jan Svankmajer has made the feature-length pieces *Faust* (1994) and *Little Otik* (2001), the latter his most outward expression of horror devices. Svankmajer's films have inspired filmmakers as diverse as Terry Gilliam, the Brothers Quay and Tim Burton, and Svankmajer has declared that 'I prefer to place my imaginary world into reality'. His adaptation of *Alice in Wonderland* uses found objects as puppets and eerily applies a very non-realistic use of sound to create a far from cute fairytale vision. It was interesting to watch the Tim Burton-directed, Disney-studio produced adaptation of Lewis Carroll's books and see if there was a glimmer of Svankmaker influence. Certainly, the film extensively combined live action and computer-animated characters to visualise Alice's coming of age, but there was little of the menace and visceral unease of the Svankmajer film. We might have to look more to Burton's production of *The Nightmare Before Christmas* (1993) for this.

It could be said that all of these Surrealist moviemaking endeavours form part of a great movie hyperlink to the film *Un Chien Andalou*, a short film which continues to fascinate audiences. It is this movie that set the tone for the dreamscapes of the Surrealist-inspired movies that followed, and which continue to be produced, creating associations and images unfettered by the constraints of realism.

Un Chien Andalou (1929)

Directed by: Luis Buñuel
Written by: Luis Buñuel and Salvador Dali
Produced by: Luis Buñuel
Edited by: Luis Buñuel
Cinematography: Duverger
Cast: Simone Mareuil (Simone), Pierre Batcheff, Luis Buñuel, Salvador Dali

Synopsis

A man is obsessed with a woman. Images of his lust for her collide with images of death and decay. There is not necessarily an inherent narrative logic at work, but instead the logic of feeling.

Concept

Buñuel and Dali spent two weeks together in early 1929. The film is named after Buñuel's first collection of poems. In 1947, Buñuel published a book about the making of the film, saying it had been conceived as a call to murder expressed in the imagery of the unconscious.

Production

Salvador Dali was only 24 when the film was produced in 1929. Luis Buñuel's mother gave her son an allowance and it was this that allowed him to pursue his Surrealist interests. Perhaps unexpectedly, Buñuel had long been a fan of American cinema and, at one time, he contributed film reviews to a range of French journals that exhibited a rounded interest in the language of cinema. *Un Chien Andalou* was developed, filmed and edited in the spring of 1929. It was filmed at a studio in Billancourt over a two-week period.

Text: Drama, Image, Sound

Un Chien Andalou combines melodrama, comedy and tragedy in a story that coheres in its own emotionally logical way as it shows a man and his desire for a woman. In the space of little more than a quarter of an hour, 300 shots play out. The film has been widely written about and is regarded as a quintessential modernist film, though it is not utterly abstract. The film has a focus on a character with a goal. In 1930, Jean Vigo championed the film as 'a film of social consciousness'.[73]

Reception and Legacy

Un Chien Andalou has achieved a kind of star status as a Surrealist film, and is one of several short films considered in this book that are as expressive and engaging as the most well-known and highly regarded feature films. A short film can often provide a very undistilled emotional impact, unimpeded by the intricacies and demands of plot. Atmosphere, feeling and theme instead prevail in a very concentrated way and the Internet has provided a fresh and expansive landscape for short films to find a home.

The film was premiered at the Studio Ursulines and was soon taken up by the Surrealists. It ran for eight months and its impact gave Buñuel an opportunity to move into feature-film production. In autumn 1929, it was paired with a Harold Lloyd comedy. In 1960, the film was revived with the addition of an integrated music track personally supervised by Buñuel (having been screened on its original release with live musical accompaniment). Like the film, the music is playfully abstract. In the UK, the film had initially been given an X-certificate and was regarded as generally too excessive for the 'ordinary' filmgoer. Writing about the film, Phil Drummond, however, advises against getting too wrapped up in the Surrealist aspects of the film, saying that 'it should not be entirely collapsed into the concerns of Surrealism at large, since the film preceded its maker's acceptance into the movement'.[74]

La Belle et la Bête (1946)

Directed by: Jean Cocteau
Written by: Jean Cocteau
Produced by: André Paulvé (Executive Producer)
Edited by: Claude Iberia
Cinematography: Henri Alekan
Cast: Jean Marais (Avenant/Beast), Josette Day (Belle), Marcel André (Belle's Father), Mila Parély (Félicie), Michel Auclair (Ludovic)

Synopsis

The handwritten opening credits acknowledge the film's fairytale source and a preamble encourages the audience to believe in the fantastical. As the credits end, we are shown the exterior of a chateau. Two young men, Ludovic and Avenant, are fooling around. Inside the chateau, we meet Belle and her two ugly sisters who are selfish and deceitful. Avenant goes to Belle and says she must not be a slave to her sisters; she should marry him instead. One night, riding through the forest, Belle's father discovers a castle that turns out to be enchanted. Exploring the castle grounds, Belle's father takes a rose and is punished for doing so by the Beast whose castle it is. As penance for the father's theft of the Beast's precious rose, the Beast tells the man he must die or that one of his daughters must die in his place. Belle's father rides home and Belle, hearing the story related by her father, decides that she will go to the castle. Avenant and Ludovic agree that they should go and kill the Beast. Enchanted by the mystery and beauty of the castle, Belle is confronted by the Beast who pledges to care for her and become her servant.

Belle informs the Beast that Avenant has asked to marry her and the Beast runs away on hearing this. Belle returns home and Avenant makes it his mission to kill the beast and secure the horde of treasures at the castle. Avenant is also determined for Belle not to return to the Beast's home and tells her that he will kill the beast so that he can free her from his hold over her. In the sanctuary of his castle the Beast feels lost without Belle, his connection to her immediate and intense. The Beast orders his magical horse, Magnificent, to ride out and collect Belle and return her to him. Magnificent reaches Belle's home but it is Avenant and Ludovic who ride it back to the Beast's castle. In turn, Belle makes her own way back to the Beast. When she arrives at the fortress she finds the Beast lying at the edge of a pond, inanimate and weak. Meanwhile, Avenant and Ludovic explore the Beast's castle and locate his horde of treasure which is protected by a statue of the goddess Diana. By the pond, Belle speaks with the Beast and he tells her that 'Beasts who love can do no more than lie down'. The Beast then dies with Belle at his side. In the Beast's treasure house, Avenant goes to steal some of his riches. At this moment, the statue of Diana awakes and fires an arrow at the intruder. The arrow strikes Avenant and he now transforms into the next iteration of the Beast. At the waterside, Belle watches as the Beast is awakened from his death; the spell on him has been broken, and he returns to his human form. Belle and her love fly to the stars.

Concept

Jean Cocteau was a Surrealist whose creative life incorporated film. *La Belle et la Bête* is one of many adaptations of the sixteenth-century French fairytale written by Madame Leprince de Beaumont. For Cocteau, cinema was an extension of writing and painting and this sensibility is powerfully evident in his rendition of the famous tale. For the press kit that was produced for the film's American release Cocteau wrote that 'when I decided to make a film that would be a fairytale, and when I chose the one that is least fairy like – which is to say the one that would need to make the least use of modern cinema's techniques – I of course knew that I was going […] against the grain […]To fairyland as people usually see it, I would bring a kind of realism...'[75]

Production

Jean Cocteau did not regard himself as a filmmaker in any kind of professional sense. Instead, he considered himself an amateur, a refreshing sensibility when we consider the term to really refer to a passionate approach to work. Indeed, this personalised approach to filmmaking perhaps partly accounts for the casting of his partner Jean Marais in the roles of both the Beast and Avenant. Cocteau was a polymath who was powerfully informed by a love of classical mythology, and this registers powerfully throughout *La Belle et la Bête*. He was a poet, a painter, a journalist, and even promoted boxing. He also wrote novels and stage plays. Cocteau's first love was theatre, and his film work possesses an engaging theatrical quality, yet one that is not staid; there is a physicality to the in-camera effects that only enhances the fantasy. The laws and lore of melodrama and fantasy, as well as the influence on Cocteau of George Méliès, underpin the film. Cocteau was 57 years old when he made *La Belle et la Bête* and he considered it to be avant-garde, consciously trying to counter the dominant visual style of the time with its mobile camera. The film's core concern is with expressing the dynamic between reality and appearance, and between life and art. Francis Steegmuller notes that 'Henri Alekan gave the photography the tone Cocteau wanted, the soft gleam of hand-polished old silver'.[76]

Cocteau went into production on the film shortly after the end of World War Two and, throughout, he was not in the best of physical health. Assistant director René Clement was a vital support for him. The film was predominantly shot on location at Rochecorbon, a seventeenth-century chateau near Tours. Exteriors of gardens were filmed at the Raray Chateau. For certain interiors, the film was based at Epinay Studios in Paris. The Delft School of painting influenced the visual design of Belle's home.

Text: Drama, Image, Sound

The film primarily celebrates true love and its redeeming power. The world of true love which Belle and the Beast eventually build for themselves is threatened by others who are not what they seem. The masks we all wear, which eventually fall away to reveal true identities, are a concern of the film. Cocteau's visual style and choices provide a mesmerising demonstration of how practical effects, achieved on set in real space and time, bestow the illusion of the fantastical with a sense of believable physicality. Perhaps the film's most startling image is of Belle re-entering her family home, seemingly through a crack in a wall. The film also invests great energy in pointing out the connections between the human and the wild, as evidenced in the balanced, near-symmetrical image of the deer statue with the Beast and Belle on either side of it.

The film's rich musical score by George Auric was one of Cocteau's favourite aspects of the finished film. Sure enough, the music lends a sense of romance, playfulness, mystery and delicacy to the images.

Reception and Legacy

Cocteau had hopes for the film to succeed in America, his ambition based on his sense that the culture that produced the writer Edgar Allan Poe, and which celebrated the childlike, would connect with his film. Certainly the film sits well alongside the affecting Disney studio adaptation of the story from 1991, and the very first words spoken by Ridley Scott in the DVD commentary for his somewhat neglected fantasy *Legend* (1985) are about *La Belle et la Bête*. 'Cocteau's fairytale,' he says, 'set standards in fantasy which few other filmmakers have reached.'[77] At the time of its original release, the film was seen as an unnecessary confection, an indulgence at a time of post-war austerity. Cocteau sensibly countered that the film was made to revive the spirit of the general audience. Film as medicine never fails to appeal and, for this writer as a child, film often possessed this kind of power.

The Tales of Hoffmann (1951)

Directed by: Michael Powell and Emeric Pressburger
Written by: Michael Powell and Emeric Pressburger
Produced by: Michael Powell and Emeric Pressburger
Edited by: Reginald Mills
Cinematography: Christopher Challis
Cast: Robert Rounseville (Hoffmann), Robert Helpmann (Lindorf/Coppelius/Dapertutto/Dr Miracle), Pamela Brown (Nicklaus), Moira Shearer (Stella/Olympia), Frederic Ashton (Kleinzach/Cochenille), Leonide Massine (Spalanzani/Schlemil/Franz), Ludmilla Tcherina (Giulietta), Anne Ayers (Antonia)

Synopsis

An orchestra tunes up and we then watch a scene from the ballet *The Dragonfly.* Viewing the performance with some intensity is the wild-eyed Councillor Lindorf, who desires the ballerina Stella. She is in love with Hoffmann, the poet who sits in the audience. During the intermission, Hoffmann goes to Luther's tavern where he talks, and finally sings, with the students who have attended the ballet. The students urge Hoffmann to tell them more stories and so he narrates three tales of women he has loved and lost. The first is the story of Olympia, who turns out to be an automaton and not a woman at all. His second doomed affair is with the courtesan, Giulietta; his third with the fragile Antonia. When Hoffmann's stories conclude, his audience of drinkers is entranced and Lindorf menacingly looks on. Hoffmann is exhausted by telling the tales and is unaware of Lindorf leaving the inn with Stella in his arms.

Concept

Michael Powell was a major, somewhat maverick figure in British cinema and perhaps only in the late 1970s, courtesy of Francis Ford Coppola and Martin Scorsese, did he enjoy a restored reputation that subsequently resulted in a widespread reconsideration and celebration of his work. His films are fantastical, attuned to the British pastoral, but with something of the mystical added in. There is general agreement that German Expressionism had a major influence on Powell, who often talked of the possibilities of a film as though it had all sorts of possibilities when thought of as composed. He ran counter to the tendency towards realism, and *Hoffmann* allows him to revel in this approach and, at times, to create a film that rather magically teeters on the brink of animation.

Powell and Pressburger embraced international influences both in their subject matter and visual style, and this set them apart somewhat from many other British-based filmmakers at the time. Michael Powell was born in Britain but Emeric Pressburger immigrated to England from Hungary and so a sense of cultural crossover was arguably inherent in his work and sense of what cinema could be. Their work adheres to a Romantic sensibility and in his book *A Cinema of Magic Spaces* Andrew Moor writes that 'Powell and Pressburger repeatedly call for actively imaginative audiences'.[78] Late in his life, Powell reflected that the film was one of the strongest he and Emeric Pressburger had produced.

Production

The Tales of Hoffmann was originally to have been shot in Germany, France, Venice and London but ultimately was all filmed at Shepperton Studios on the edge of London. A choice was also made to stage much of the action as ballet, and the film is a florid manifestation of Powell and Pressburger's romantic inclinations. Alexander Korda gave Powell and Pressburger much creative freedom. It was the conductor Sir Thomas Beecham who had originally suggested a movie based on Offenbach's opera *The Tales of Hoffmann*. Ian Christie calls the film 'the absolute antithesis of realism'.[79] In making *The Tales of Hoffmann*, Powell was able to pursue his dream of what he called the 'composed film', one 'in which sound and image would be as closely integrated as they normally are in animation'.[80]

The film was produced entirely in the studio environment. Production designer Hein Heckroth oversaw the creation of sculptural elements and other arresting practical visual 'effects' and the film's music score was recorded first and played live on set to be performed to. Because the film was effectively silent, not anchored to synchronously recorded dialogue, Powell used differing camera speeds.

Text: Drama, Image, Sound

The film is a dance film and it is replete with expressionist devices and a wilful countering of any sense of realism. Its sequences are playful and often quite frightening. The final image of the film shows the libretto being shut and stamped with the words 'Made in England'. The film, just as with Powell and Pressburger's other work, foregrounds aspects of its artifice.

The film revels in its musical form and, perhaps more than anything, its message is that we need stories; we love their artifice. The tale of Olympia, colour coded around yellows and purples, tells of how Hoffmann falls in love with a beautiful young woman. Seduced into a relationship with her by her 'father', Hoffmann finally realises that Olympia is only an automaton. The story, then, is about the relationship between humans and technology and the story ends with comically horrific destruction. The character of the inventor Coppelius is wonderfully odd and menacing.

Throughout the film there is no claim to a surface realism but, instead, a commitment to capturing the realism of emotion in a way that echoes and anticipates Dali and Buñuel, Svankmajer and the Quays. The three tales that Hoffmann narrates all explore the destructive effects of passion and lust. In the second story, the tale of Giulietta, the colour of a dark, maroon red defines the setting. This is a decadent world, a kind of hell or Hades, and, from the start, Powell's fascination with the classical world is evident. The physicality of the illusion-making connects the film to Cocteau's *La Belle et la Bête*, notably in the scene where Dapertutto changes candle wax into a jewel with which to seduce Giulietta. This second tale is ripe with obsessive behaviour as Dapertutto charges Giulietta with the task of capturing Hoffmann's reflection (or, rather, his soul, for Dapertutto is a collector of souls). Once it has been taken, Hoffmann duels with another man, Schlemil, who has also lost his soul to Giulietta.

The third story, the tale of Antonia, sees Antonia overwhelmed by the machinations of Dr Miracle who exploits Antonia's love for her late mother, finally encouraging her to sing herself to death.

Dr Miracle is surely one of the most frightening-looking villains ever, a more intense version of Dr Caligari fused with Nosferatu. Certainly, the film might well be Robert Helpmann's as he plays the villainous force throughout. This sense of Helpmann as the centre of everything in the film is supported by a point made by Janet Leeper, in 1944, in her book *English Ballet* when she writes, 'Helpmann's sense of the theatre is so great that it outweighs his technical qualifications. He is never dull. Every part is a part for him.'[81]

The film's transitions and in-camera and optical effects are fascinating and there is no attempt made at any kind of photorealism, which liberates the filmmaker and the viewer. Instead, a romantic beauty and sense of a world in decay pervade. There is a beautiful image of Hoffmann on a little boat rowing towards the island on which Antonia and her father, Crespel, live, amidst the classical ruins of their home.

In an essay about the film, Ian Christie, the world authority on Powell's career, wrote that, 'What makes the film so remarkable is a series of paradoxes: the fact that it virtually reinvented the freedom and fantasy of silent cinema while making full use of Technicolor and a stellar cast of dancers and singers; and that by remaining faithful to an 1880 opera, Powell and Pressburger managed to make a highly personal film […] about the fate of the artist.'[82]

La règle du jeu: Love, loyalty and the power of art find a home in a country house

Kes: Nature's power awakens a young boy's vision

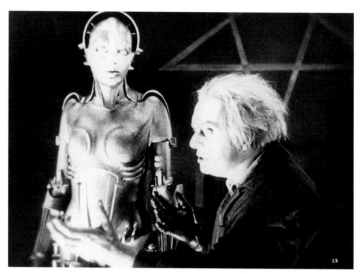

Metropolis: A crucible in which science, ambition, imagination and power collide

The Passion of Joan of Arc: Beauty confronts the beasts

The Seventh Seal: Stark hearts and death's shadow strike a blow of stunning seriousness to the historical movie

The Man Who Planted Trees: Lyricism and the spirit of generosity in motion

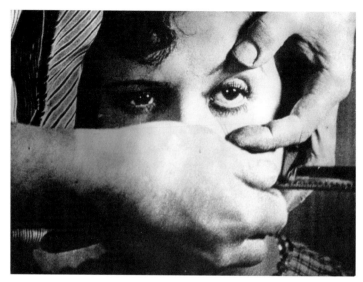

Un Chien Andalou: Dreamscapes of the everyday

La Belle et la Bête: A decorous delight in re-imagining a realm of wonder

Koyaanisqatsi: Documentary film as epic poem and chant

Into Great Silence: Where watching a film becomes mesmerising meditation

Pan's Labyrinth: Where fairytale's shadows provide escape and illumination

Jules et Jim: The sorrows of growing up seem so remote

Seven Samurai: The power of community was never more vividly imagined

Picnic at Hanging Rock: Where the wild things are and the civilised things are not

The Man With the Movie Camera: The joy of moviemaking, the thrill of city living

Atanarjuat: The Fast Runner: The ancient tales endure

Reception and Legacy

The film was premiered in America at New York City's Metropolitan Opera House on 11 April 1951. In the UK, the film was the first Royal Film Performance and Andrew Moor has noted that the press often connected the film to the Festival of Britain. These two situations aside, the film was not readily embraced by audiences, though a later British filmmaker, Derek Jarman, is widely regarded as having been informed by the film's costume design.

The Tales of Hoffmann is rightly regarded as being almost a horror film, and certainly George Romero and Martin Scorsese have spoken of their admiration for it. When the film was released, it was reviewed as follows in the UK publication *Monthly Film Bulletin*: 'The total ensemble of striving romanticism, of Offenbach, of expressionist theatrical decors [...] of rich Technicolor photography, of simultaneous opera and ballet [...] results more in overwhelming confusion even than incongruity.'[83]

THE DOCUMENTARY VISION

Documentary as truth might be one of the great lies of cinema. Documentary scholar Bill Nichols has made the claim that all films are documentaries and he may well be on to something. This book can only hint at the vast range of documentary filmmakers who have produced such fascinating material. Certainly, it can only indicate in the most cursory way what the documentary mode is about.

Let's start with some fundamental ways in which the documentary form can be distinguished from the 'fiction' form. In the book *An Introduction to Film Studies* we see the documentary defined as follows: 'It is in the aesthetic concerns of documentary that there is considerable debate, because it is largely in creating an aesthetic approach that documentaries and other non-fiction films begin to challenge, distort, and subvert notions of "documentary" truth and "authenticity."'[84]

It seems right to suggest that the films of the Lumière Brothers, as well as many other titles from Britain's cinema-of-attractions output during the very earliest years of the twentieth century, could be regarded as documentary. Stella Bruzzi has suggested that the history of documentaries is misunderstood, depicting as it often does the idea that one kind of documentary exists and flourishes until another comes along to replace it. For Bruzzi, however, this is too neat a scheme of things.[85]

The world of documentary has a long tradition and inevitably has its *auteurs* and major players. Names such as Robert Flaherty,

Albert Maysles, Maya Deren, Errol Morris, Molly Dineen, Chris Marker, Nick Broomfield, Godfrey Reggio and Frederick Wiseman all offer potent stories of 'real' life. Indeed, we might want to cite the Lumière brothers in late-nineteenth-century Paris as the instigators of the form with films such as their micro-movie *Workers leaving the Lumière Factory* (1895). The Lumière films can be described as a 'cinema of attractions' where narrative traditions and characterisation have yet to play their part. 'Unplayed' is the term a Soviet filmmaker might have used at one time.

For the culturally embedded, broadly understood use of the word 'documentary' we have to thank the British filmmaker John Grierson. He minted the word when reviewing the film *Moana* (1925), directed by Robert Flaherty, observing that the job of the documentary was 'the creative treatment of reality'.

Adding critical, theoretic ballast to the idea of the documentary mode (and underscoring the importance of theory and practice sitting side by side), filmmaker Dziga Vertov observed that, 'The cameraman uses many specific devices to "attack" reality with his camera and to put the facts together in a new structure; these devices help him to strive for a better world with more perceptive people.'[86]

Like the 'fiction' film, the 'documentary' has its own language which has established itself as a set of conventions. Certainly, Robert Flaherty's use of the long lens allowed him to maintain some physical distance from his subjects so that they could go about their business without being conscious of the camera in their immediate vicinity. However, Flaherty's film *Nanook of the North* (1922) also re-staged events that Flaherty recalled from earlier journeys north to Hudson Bay in 1910 and 1916. Whereas the Eskimos had hunted using guns, Flaherty replaced them with traditional, outmoded weapons. The authenticity of the documentary is therefore thrown perilously into question very early in its life. Where Flaherty offered humanist, people-specific films, John Grierson favoured a more overtly political approach and subject matter, and this came to underpin the *cinema vérité* style that the Maysles Brothers always referred to as 'direct cinema'; that is to say, cinema of minimal artifice in its construction, therefore implying immediacy and, by extension, accuracy and honesty. These words are easy to write but, given a moment's thought, prove contentious and open the portal to a ravenous philosophical dimension surrounding truth and art.

In their landmark book *Film Art: An Introduction* (arguably *the* place to start any serious film study), David Bordwell and Kristin Thompson write of documentary that: 'Like fiction films, documentaries also have their own genres.'[87] They also make the point that documentary's claim to some kind of absolute truth is questionable, saying that even a fiction film has some kind of connection to the actual world.

Another variation on the idea of the documentary is the movement that has come to be called Third Cinema. This is a form of guerilla cinema based around group production, with the emphasis on distribution and screening rather than aesthetic choices. Third Cinema has been couched in the following context: 'The anti-imperialist struggle of the people of the Third World and of their equivalents inside the imperialist countries constitutes today the axis of the world revolution.'[88]

Typically, documentary is regarded as more truthful than fiction, but the evidence seems to suggest otherwise: it's just as much of a construct. Thomas Austin talks about the limiting cliché of the window on the world.

Bill Nichols wrote that 'documentary is a fiction (un)like any other'.[89] There's a wrong-headed sense that a documentary is more virtuous than something 'made up' but, having worked on a number of documentaries and information films whilst in my twenties, I can testify to just how much the material is organised, selected and manipulated. With a fiction film, the majority of these choices are perhaps made during the screenwriting stage, whilst in documentary this tends to happen during post-production.

In recent years, films such as *Roger and Me* (Michael Moore, 1989), *Grizzly Man* (Werner Herzog, 2005), *Into Great Silence* (Philip Gröning, 2005), *Tell Them Who You Are* (Mark Wexler, 2004),

Being and Doing (Ken McMullen, 1984) and *March of the Penguins* (Luc Jacquet, 2005) have all been theatrical releases which have reconfirmed documentary's status as 'cinema', distinguished by an arresting diversity of subject matter and treatment. Critically, in terms of the very small number of films referenced here as documentary, they all take a viewpoint, revelling in their subjectivity. There is not an ambition to somehow tell both sides of a given story. As such the films are arguably as intensively rendered and authored as films such as *The Seventh Seal*, *Seven Samurai* or *Rome, Open City*.

Koyaanisqatsi (1982)

Directed by: Godfrey Reggio
Written by: Godfrey Reggio
Produced by: Godfrey Reggio
Edited by: Ron Fricke and Anton Walpole
Cinematographer: Ron Fricke

Synopsis

Koyaanisqatsi tours the modern western world of cities and industry, offering images and sequences that suggest points of conflict and tension between what is natural and what is artificial. The associational narrative structure, comprising images connected by a theme, means the film can be viewed on a loop.

Concept

Over the past ten years the documentary feature film has enjoyed a popular resurgence, pushing it confidently towards the mainstream audience. However, in the 1980s, alongside the monumental and elegant work of Ken Burns, rooted in archival material, voice-over and interviews, creating a sense of national folk memory, and the investigative journalism of Errol Morris in films such as *The Thin Blue Line* (1988), another documentary maker emerged on the scene: Godfrey Reggio.

Reggio's work is marked by his background in public information media and his early adult life as a monk. His films possess a meditative quality. In the mid-1970s, through community work and media, Reggio began to recognise the power of the moving image and started to work with it. In 1982, he released *Koyaanisqatsi* with Francis Ford Coppola 'presenting' the film as executive producer. This was followed in 1988 by *Powaqqatsi*, with the support of Coppola and George Lucas. Finally, in 2004, there was the third in the trilogy, *Naqoyqatsi*, which was presented by Steven Soderbergh. Of this body of work Reggio has said, 'I realise fully that any meaning or value *Koyaanisqatsi* might have comes exclusively from the beholder. [...] This is the highest value of any work of art, not predetermined meaning, but meaning gleaned from the experience of the encounter.'[90] The word *koyaanisqatsi* means 'life out of balance', implying that there is a disjuncture between the urban/technological and nature. The title *Powaqqatsi* means 'life in transformation'. According to Godfrey Reggio, 'these films are meant to provoke'[91] in their examination of the world beyond its immediate surface realities. One of the key influences on Reggio was *Los Olvidados* (1950) by Luis Buñuel.

Production

Reggio's interest in 'socially engaged' filmmaking probably stems in part from his very earliest experiences working for the Institute for Regional Education (IRE) where he directed a 'non-narrative' film. The IRE went on to produce *Koyaanisqatsi* and footage for the film was gathered in the late 1970s and early 1980s. In due course, film director and producer Francis Ford Coppola saw the film and became its 'presenter'.

Text: Drama, Image, Sound

Koyaanisqatsi is about neither an individual nor a localised situation. The film is sombre and its first image connects our modern world to that of the ancients as we are shown an image of a Hopi wall painting. On the soundtrack we hear the word *koyaanisqatsi* being chanted. For anyone who knows the grand vistas of Ansel Adams's photography, the film contains a range of images that will reverberate with familiarity. The prologue is built around images of the American desert in something of an overture. The film then goes on to present images of fire and steel and also of a spaceship launching. The shapes of landscape are vital. The film doesn't identify or label places and the absence of voice-over or context supports the film's meditative power. Stillness and speed are placed in powerful opposition.

Throughout, the film presents its share of apocalyptic images and those of slow-moving crowds are sluggish and doom laden.

Some of the images in the film must have so settled into the wider culture that what would once have seemed fresh now seems a little more conventional. For example, the image of a setting sun reflected in the window of a skyscraper is powerful and poetic but also very familiar to us. In many ways, the film echoes the work of Dziga Vertov in his film *The Man With the Movie Camera* (1929). Like that much earlier film, *Koyaanisqatsi* is not based around a theatrical, dramatic mode. It is a sensory experience rather than a narrative one.

Amidst the grand vistas of technology and nature, there are many portrait shots of groups and individuals, notably the USAF pilot against his plane, camera pushing in slow motion to surround him with the darkness of a fighter-plane engine.

In a thrilling way, the film is exhausting, but maybe that is the point. Amidst the growing sense of a world bereft of individual experience, the film finds moments that jar, such as the unexpected sight of a man shaving his face whilst standing on a hectic city-street corner. Menace underpins certain moments of the film, memorably when the *koyaanisqatsi* chant and organ accompanies images of flaming spaceship debris falling to earth.

The film's sequel, *Powaqqatsi*, opens with percussive, aggressive yet playful, music-tracking images of a mine filled with hundreds of men at work. It is an image that suggests a world before mechanisation occurred. The composer Philip Glass recorded the music for the film prior to the start of shooting. This was then given to the camera crews so that they could listen to it and time their moves to the music. Humans are repeatedly seen as tiny, almost insignificant figures against the mighty landscape. The bright colours of fabric and costume contrast with the earthy colours, and the performance of rituals runs as a strong motif throughout.

There is a startling image of little girl in a pink dress standing on the right edge of the frame with graffiti about war and fighting behind her. She just looks at the camera.

One of the film's emblematic scenes shows a boy walking along a rough, hard roadside with a huge truck and a swirl of dust engulfing him, threatening him. This image was resonant enough to become the film's theatrical release poster.

Reception and Legacy

The film has influenced *Winged Migration* (Jacques Perrin, 2001), *Microcosmos* (Claude Nuridsany, 1996), *Baraka* (Ron Fricke, 1992) and *March of the Penguins* (Luc Jacquet, 2005). When *Koyaanisqatsi* was released it received very positive reviews that identified the film's aesthetic of 'pure' cinema style, and also its attempt to create relationships between shots, scenes and sequences that would prompt audiences to question and make connections. It's a film that stands as a useful example of film as philosophy.

Night Mail (1936)

Directed by: Harry Watt
Written by: WH Auden
Produced by: Harry Watt and Basil Wright
Edited by: Basil Wright
Cinematographer: HE Fowle

Synopsis

Night Mail is a documentary that charts the overnight journey of the postal train service from London to Glasgow, ensuring the timely delivery of mail to the population of Scotland. The film's first phase documents the start of the route with stations being readied and post loaded onto the train. The middle section offers an insight into the working of the 40 men on the train whose job is to sort the mail en route. The final third centres on WH Auden's voice-over poem, which accompanies images of the train hurtling towards its destination.

Concept

Night Mail was an information film commissioned by the General Post Office to explain the London to Glasgow service to its staff. The film is a key moment in the sequence of British documentary filmmaking that ran from the mid-1920s to the mid-1940s and which had as its critical focus the General Post Office Film Unit of 1933–9. John Grierson got several writers to take the journey and record their impressions. The first cut dealt only with the mechanics of the operation; there was nothing about the people. Subsequently, WH Auden wrote the verse to humanise the proceedings and Benjamin Britten composed the effervescent music.

Production

Night Mail is the pleasing result of an endeavour to make an information film, a documentary of the humblest kind, perhaps, and to make it as entertaining and filled with human interest as possible. In doing so, it is a *very* constructed documentary, again urging us to approach with caution the idea of documentary film as somehow more real than, and maybe even morally superior to, all of those made-up fictions and wish fulfilments and happy-ending films. At the General Post Office they had two divisions producing information films about their work and services. One unit was dedicated to fairly 'mundane' projects and the other to more experimental approaches. *Night Mail* was produced by the latter.

The film was directed by Harry Watt with the screenplay written by Basil Wright. John Grierson and Stuart Legg were also involved and it is arguably Grierson's name that remains most synonymous with the film. Grierson had been so central to the development of the documentary mode in British cinema and culture in the 1930s, engaged and interested as he was by the political landscape of the country at the time, and expressing a particular interest in the Red Clydeside political movement. (As an aside, Grierson had been involved in the editing and presentation of Eisenstein's Soviet Montage movie *Battleship Potemkin*.)

Text: Drama, Image, Sound

Night Mail celebrates the British regions in a way that is almost exultant once the Down Postal Special train breaks free of the bonds of London. The film contrasts rural, wide-sky Britain with the worlds of the urban and the industrial, and also quietly celebrates the working man and the routines and disciplines of his life. Certain images hold fast in the memory: the silhouette of the mine machinery and that of the postal-train worker leaning out of the train. Then, too, there is the abrupt cut contrasting the fast speed of the train with the slow and deliberate pace of a farmer leading his horse across a yard.

The images are accompanied by percussive, repetitive musical lines (courtesy of Benjamin Britten) and the film celebrates not only the postal service but plainly reminds us how photogenic trains in motion pictures are. Another feature the film focuses on is the rapidity with which communication is possible in the modern world, and it could be said that the film enshrines the moment when the rapid transit information age began to embed itself in Britain. *Night Mail* is characterised by a modest sense of wonder at it all and takes real delight in creating images of the regions of England and Scotland. In an essay about the British documentary, Ian Aitken summarises the Grierson view of documentary as being 'to promote an understanding of social and cultural connections within the nation'.[92]

Reception and Legacy

Night Mail was one of the most commercially successful documentaries ever produced. Upon its release, it was described by *Monthly Film Bulletin* thus: 'The commentator recites verses in time with the train's rhythm, romanticises the object of the journey...'[93]

Nanook of the North (1922)

Directed by: Robert Flaherty
Written by: Robert Flaherty
Produced by: Robert Flaherty
Edited by: Robert Flaherty
Cinematography: Robert Flaherty
Cast: Nanook, Nyla, Cunayo, Allee, Allegoo

Synopsis

The film charts the experiences of an Inuit family as they live their lives amidst the seemingly inhospitable surroundings of the Arctic. It begins with Nanook preparing to leave camp and trade with the white traders. We see him meeting with a white man who shows Nanook how a record player operates. A series of intertitles across the film constructs a range of contexts. Nanook is described as a member of 'the kindly, brave, simple Eskimo'. The film describes itself as 'a story of life and love in the actual Arctic... the fearless, happy-go-lucky Eskimo.' The film is set around Hopewell Sound and the Itivimuit tribe. The first shot of Nanook shows him looking directly at the camera. Nanook is shown capturing food for the near starving tribe and we see him going about the routines of daily life:

hunting, making an igloo, preparing the kayak for travel. The film shows Nanook and others on their dogsleds and then racing to get to safety as a 'threatening drifter drives in'.

Concept

Nanook was the result of what Flaherty perceived as a filmmaking error. He had been on an expedition to the North (Canada) as part of a mining expedition and took with him, at the prompting of an associate, a film camera to document the journey. When Flaherty returned home and reviewed the footage, disappointment set in as he realised he had made a very dull film with no human interest. 'My wife and I thought it over for a long time... Why not take a typical Eskimo and his family and make a biography of their lives through a year?'[94] Flaherty's epiphany set the project that became *Nanook* in motion.

When Flaherty approached film producers with his proposed subject there were no takers. Instead, Flaherty took the independent route and secured financing from Revillon Frères, a French fur company with business interests in Canada. Pathé's American office distributed the film, which went on to become an iconic documentary even though much of it was re-staged and re-enacted for the camera, thereby forever throwing the concept of documentary as truth into disrepute. Filming, on the eastern shore of Hudson Bay, took two years and Flaherty did all the camera work himself. Of his experience, Flaherty observed that '[Nanook] never understood why I should have gone to all the fuss and bother...'[95]

Robert Flaherty has often been criticised for his film's lack of authenticity, but perhaps documentaries are closer to fiction than we think. As John Grierson commented, documentary is defined by the creative interpretation of reality. Flaherty was also criticised for not engaging enough with 'hard' subjects – gritty reality – instead choosing a kind of rural, pastoral subject.

Production

The production of Nanook was surely an adventure in itself. It took two months for Flaherty to travel from New York to the east side of Hudson Bay via canoe and schooner. With him, Flaherty had two motion-picture cameras, film-processing equipment and film-projection equipment. Once having established a base in Eskimo country, Flaherty had to build a processing hut, using wood collected by his Eskimo hosts for the construction. Flaherty would project rushes for the Eskimos to view.

Text: Drama, Image, Sound

The film comprises many elegantly composed shots. Viewing the film, one is aware of the degrees to which its scenes have been staged and re-set for 'maximum' entertainment and engagement value.

As fascinating, and often otherworldly, as the images are, the series of intertitles that establish scenes attest to the degree to which the film is a construct. Much of the tone of the intertitles conjures up the feeling of an adventure novel, something reliant on spectacle and the extraordinary feats of an individual. Hence, we read statements such as, 'Upon his skill in traversing dangerous ice floes his success depends.' The film talks of 'the melancholy spirit of the North'. So much for documentary being somehow cool headed and stripped of artifice.

The film utilises familiar techniques from 'dramatic narrative fiction' films in recreating and re-staging aspects of Eskimo life. For example, when Nanook goes to catch a seal, the fact that the seal, although we know it is there, cannot be seen beneath the ice lends the scene added tension. As such, the scene trades on the construction of an unseen entity in much the same way as a film like *Jaws* (Steven Spielberg, 1975).

Nanook of the North ultimately proves most compelling in the way that it shows often mundane daily tasks in a captivating way, simply by staying with them rather than editing for only the most 'interesting' parts. This willingness to dwell and linger puts the film on a similar course to a documentary such as *Into Great Silence*.

Reception and Legacy

With the film eventually completed, Flaherty took it to Pathé, but they wanted to distribute and exhibit it as a series of educational films rather than as a unified, single feature. Flaherty held fast to his ambition for it to be shown as one film and the film was finally screened alongside Harold Lloyd's feature-length comedy debut, *Grandma's Boy*, in New York City. Response to *Nanook* in America was muted. When it screened in London, Paris and Berlin, however, the film was very warmly received.

Nanook was criticised for its imagery of the 'noble savage' and for presenting an idyllic view of a particular culture. Indeed, the film largely reconstructs, rather than records, a lifestyle that had in fact disappeared. The children shown as Nanook's in the film were not his children. Just a year after filming was completed, Nanook died of starvation.

The film paved the way for the development of ethnographic filmmaking and Flaherty continued to work in this mode. Reviews of the film have included this celebratory comment from Roger Ebert: 'Nanook stands alone in its stark regard for the courage and ingenuity of its heroes.'[96]

Shoah (1985)

Directed by: Claude Lanzmann
Written by: Claude Lanzmann
Produced by: Claude Lanzmann
Edited by: Ziva Postec
Cinematography: Dominique Chapuis, Jimmy Glasberg, William Luptchansky

Synopsis

Shoah is an immense, nine-hour documentary of testimonies about the Holocaust.

Concept

Claude Lanzmann is considered a major post-World War Two cultural figure and he has displayed a lifelong commitment to the interview-based documentary. The word *Shoah* means chaos or annihilation and Lanzmann felt compelled to build his film around the testimonies of camp survivors and also unwitting former guards who were not aware they were being filmed.

Production

Shoah was the culmination of eight years of research and gathering of testimony. Among the challenges facing the production team was how to achieve the secret filming of former SS soldiers. At one point, the crew were found out and Lanzmann was hospitalised for eight days.

Lanzmann has noted that: 'When I started this film, I had to deal with, on the one hand, the disappearance of the traces: there was nothing at all, sheer nothingness…'[97] In the end, however, he found several dozen survivors to interview and gathered around 350 hours of testimony.

Text: Drama, Image, Sound

Stella Bruzzi has observed that Lanzmann's frequent appearances on screen in the documentary are important, for they make the film very much about his personal discovery of the tragedy; his confrontation and engagement with it therefore seem that much more vivid. The film is marked, too, by moments when the testimonies give way to unsettling images of the camps as they were in the 1980s.

Regarding what gives the film its particular resonance, it is useful to quote Stella Bruzzi again at this point. She writes that, 'The film's power stems in part from the central journey being both metaphorical and actual, both concerned with the emotional and intellectual comprehension of the Holocaust and with its physical organisation and execution.'[98]

In terms of its structure, *Shoah* does not follow a linear chronology but is more about building a multitude of impressions and memories of the events related. At the risk of sounding crass, we could compare the film to *Wings of Desire* (1987), which is also about memory, both individual and collective.

A simple choice, but an effective one, was for the film not to be anchored by any kind of contextualising voice over and Lanzmann's decision not to tell personal stories so much as to give a sense of the immensity of the annihilation.

Reception and Legacy

Shoah premiered in Paris in April 1985 and was massively successful in every respect. Simone de Beauvoir wrote of the film that its 'subtle construction calls to mind... a musical composition'.[99]

At a very specific level of detail, an image from *Shoah* – of a train driver smiling as he draws his finger across his neck – was used by Steven Spielberg in the film *Schindler's List* (1993). In an essay by Yoshifa Loshitzky, we read that, 'If, indeed, Spielberg "stole" Lanzmann's visual signature, then we might talk about a relationship of envy, based on an attempt to appropriate and assimilate one's object of envy. If, on the other hand, Spielberg used "Lanzmann's image" as an homage quotation, then we may talk about a relationship of pure admiration in which the master's influence is acknowledged.'[100]

Lanzmann subsequently made the documentary *Sobidor* (2001), centred on a Jewish revolt and escape from a concentration camp.

Into Great Silence (2008)

Directed by: Philip Gröning
Produced by: Philip Gröning
Edited by: Philip Gröning
Cinematography: Philip Gröning

Synopsis

Into Great Silence is structured around a calendar year in the life of La Grande Chartreuse monastery in the French Alps. Threading through the film are aspects of the experience of a novice monk, named Benjamin, as he engages with the routines and disciplines of a hard monastic life. We see the monks at prayer, both alone and together, we see meals being prepared, administration being undertaken, walks being enjoyed, gardening being done; and threading through all of these 'ordinary' tasks is the turning of the seasons and a very clear sense of the spiritual, contemplative life. The filmmaking is as unadorned as the way of life that it portrays.

Concept

Philip Gröning has said of the film's genesis that it moved from being a film that might have explored the subject of time's passing (a fairly abstract subject, we might say) and instead settled on something more concrete: 'At the beginning, it wasn't so much the idea of shooting a film on life in a monastery; instead, I had wanted to make a film concerning the moment of time. Only later did the idea take hold of me to make a movie on life in a monastery.'[101]

Production

Philip Gröning had originally asked permission to film at La Grande Chartreuse monastery in 1984, but it wasn't until 16 years after his initial approach that the General Prior of the monastery granted him access, with the proviso that there would be no other crew in attendance. The only other time that the monastery – but not the monks – had been recorded on film was in 1960. Gröning lived at the monastery for six months and shot 120 hours of film, immersing himself in the life he wanted to depict the essence of.

Text: Drama, Image, Sound

If one needed almost unquestionable evidence of the relationship between form and content, that style is meaning, then *Into Great Silence* would serve that need. The film is built around the timeframe of a calendar year; of the changing seasons. This movement of nature is placed against the order of the monastery. The camera remains locked off and static for periods of time. We tend to think of so many films being fast and skittish now, but this film is intensely slow and utterly powerful. *Into Great Silence* reels you in and, appropriately, puts you into something of a trance. The film seems to become one with its subject matter, assuming the quality of a meditation. There is no voice-over, no sense of the history or context of the monastery, only the sense of a relatively specific timeframe. The film uses synchronous sound and delights in the shuffling of feet along corridors, the slamming of doors, the silence of the monks' cells. There are no interviews with the monks either. One elderly monk does talk about his faith and conception of death but it is not in the form of an interview.

This is an immersing and beautiful piece of work, so organised and ordered and constructed, yet feeling immediate, and with a plain, unfussy quality to it. There's a maturity to the film in that it trusts you to have the faith to stay with it and understand some of the demands of a spiritual life. It demands patience on the part of the viewer.

The film uses available light and, throughout, there are images of sunlight filling hallways and the monks' cells.

Gröning has observed: 'I did not want to shoot a film about the monastery, but a film about being a monk. Especially since I also see parallels here to the life of an artist. And to my everyday life as a filmmaker. I am concerned about the many sacrifices one makes because of the things one wants to do, and how one consistently pushes away certain other things. In both worlds, we are dealing with concepts such as concentration, perception, the meaning of doing.'[102]

Reception and Legacy

The film received very positive reviews acknowledging that it went beyond being just a film, becoming an experience in and of itself; a spiritual film about dwelling in a particular moment. This work would sit well with André Bazin and his conception of the filmmaker's having faith in reality as discussed at the very beginning of the book. The *Guardian* described the film in relation to paintings, noting that 'the dark interior images bring to mind the paintings of Velazquez's contemporary, Francisco Zurbaran, who specialised in austere, realistic portraits of monks and saints at prayer and was in fact employed by a Carthusian monastery in Spain in the 1630s'.[103]

We Are the Lambeth Boys (1952)

Directed by: Karel Reisz
Written by: Karel Reisz
Produced by: Leon Clore
Edited by: John Fletcher
Cinematography: Walter Lassally
Music: Johnny Dankworth

Synopsis

The film documents events around the Alford House youth club in Lambeth. We meet the main clubbers and their time at the youth club is contrasted with their working lives and then with a visit to a north London private school for a game of cricket. A voice-over narrates the events as they unfold.

Concept

Free Cinema was an overtly politically and socially committed filmmaking movement with a mission to represent the everyday. Cinema never tires of capturing images of youth. From *I Vitelloni* (1953) to *The Kid* (1921), from *American Graffiti* (1973) to *Pinocchio* (1940), the list is immense. *We Are the Lambeth Boys* is one of several well regarded and significant documentaries that played their part in laying the blueprint for the evolution of British social-realist cinema. The key figures of Free Cinema were Lorenza Marretti, Karel Reisz, Walter Lassally, John Fletcher, Lindsay Anderson and Tony Richardson.

Karel Reisz, who directed the film, stated that his approach to cinema was 'a question of filming based much more on observation than on abstraction'.[101] Given the artfulness of the Free Cinema movement, it is astonishing that it remains somewhat neglected, given how important it was to a wider sense of what cinema could do in a British cultural and social context.

Production

Like many movements, Free Cinema burned brightly over a relatively short period of time in the 1950s. Certainly it was a tributary that fed into the larger stream of social realism in literature and theatre. Free Cinema endeavoured to exist outside of the mainstream British film industry – free from profit-driven production and free from studio involvement – and it was a movement committed to author-led (highly constructed) cinema documentary, underwritten by American financiers such as Walter Reade. Later in their careers, Anderson, Reisz and Richardson would all go on to make narrative fiction movies. *We Are the Lambeth Boys* was shot in the south London borough of Lambeth where, in some ways, the sense of disenfranchised youth that it depicts still endures.

Text: Drama, Image, Sound

Jaunty music by Johnny Dankworth helps set the mood as the camera pans over a council estate and picks up two boys en route to the youth club. A very middle-class narrator introduces us to the young people. Regarding the youth club, he says, 'more like it are needed.' This is therefore a film with a civic purpose, i.e. to show the benefits of youth clubs. Is some of the material staged, such as the girls clustered and chatting? 'A chat and a giggle for the girls and a bit of cricket in the nets for the boys,' says the voice-over. It all seems very naïve now. The narrator talks patronisingly of 'the rowdy generation' and the film is marred throughout by a sense of condescension, even though its overriding intention seems to be to enlighten its (original) audience with regard to the positive ways in which young people can be viewed. Contrast the use of voice-over here with the absence of voice-over in the documentary *Into Great Silence.* Alongside sequences of the young people at the club, we are also shown scenes of them in their working lives and several at school. We see younger boys at school, singing in assembly, and the film carries the sound of the hymn being sung over images of some of the older teenagers at work. There's a kind of poetic realism at work that readily found a place in British realist cinema in the ensuing years – witness, for example, *The Loneliness of the Long Distance Runner* (1962).

Reception and Legacy

The Free Cinema movement is still relatively little known despite its impact as a precursor to the burgeoning social-realist commitment of British cinema in the 1960s. It anticipated and informed the social-realist drama films of the 1960s such as *Saturday Night and Sunday Morning* (1960). The films' release on DVD has made the material more readily available and, as historical documents about very specific experiences and lives, they are mesmerising. Of the Free

Cinema output, the writer John Berger observed that 'one thinks again about Documentary as an art form'.[104]

SOVIET MONTAGE

Prior to the evolution towards montage, Soviet cinema had tended to focus on melodramas where acting was the focal point. For the montage filmmakers, however, exclusively cinematic devices of cinema were the focus. By the time the First World War ended in 1918, the Russian economy was hard pressed to cover the cost of elaborate film production and so limitations had to be turned to the filmmaker's advantage. The period of Soviet Montage is typically understood to have run from 1924 until 1930, a concentrated moment in time that saw the formal and ideological dynamics of a certain kind of cinema become defined. The government in Russia took control of film production via the Commission of Education and, critically, they limited the amount of film stock made available to filmmakers. As such, a limitation ultimately proved a boon, as limitations often do. A new kind of visual inventiveness was required to make the most out of the scanty resources. Dziga Vertov busied himself compiling documentary footage of the Russian Revolution of 1917 and Lev Kuleshov worked as a teacher at the State School of Cinema Art where he explored the capacities of editing. In 1920, Sergei Eisenstein, perhaps the name now most synonymous with Soviet Montage, worked on the propaganda train which went out to Russian troops in combat in the Civil War. In this same year, Eisenstein also worked with the Proletkult Theatre in Moscow.

It was in 1924 that Soviet Montage began to glimmer via a screening at the State Film School of Lev Kuleshov's *The Extraordinary*

Adventures of Mr West in the Land of the Bolsheviks. Montage flourished but the movement was over by the early-1930s, thanks to the influence of a government that wanted films to be more socially realistic. Where Pudovkin wanted to use editing to create very neat and ordered sequences, Eisenstein was of the view that a certain sense of chaos and disorder in editing patterns – or a lack of pattern, rather – would have a more powerful effect on audiences. For Eisenstein, highly individualised characters were not essential: the stronger, overarching concept was to portray society as the character. Despite the vivid expression that montage allowed, however, the government ultimately viewed it as too abstract and alienating a device for the mass audience; too elitist and esoteric.

Although Sergei Eisenstein was regarded for many years as the major force behind the montage movement, in more recent times his oeuvre has been treated with somewhat less reverence, and VF Perkins discredits montage and its lack of subtlety in *Film as Film*. Eisenstein started out as an engineer rather than as an artist, and this background explains much about the qualities of his work. He served in the Red Army and then worked in Proletkult Workers Theatre Group before moving into film. In quick succession he made *Strike* (1924), *Battleship Potemkin* (1926) and *October* (1927), all of which enshrine the montage idea. In 1925, Eisenstein went to Hollywood and tried to mount a feature adaptation of Dreiser's novel *An American Tragedy*, but the project was never realised. Eisenstein returned to Russia in 1937 but was unable to re-enter the cinema culture as before.

Strike (1924) tells the story of an uprising of factory workers against their bosses, famously employing montage to express fairly heavy-handed political ideas. The slaying of the workers is intercut with images of a bull being slaughtered.

Soviet Montage remains a vital force that is frequently referenced in modern films. The climax of the Hollywood period thriller *The Untouchables* (1987) builds tension around a baby carriage hurtling down a staircase, a spectacle that overtly recalls a famous sequence from *Battleship Potemkin*. We might also suggest that the rapid pace of montage editing finds its modern equivalent and evolution in action movies, and even more so in movie trailers. *REF*

The Man With the Movie Camera
(Chevlovek s kinoapparaton) (1929)

Directed by: Dziga Vertov
Written by: Dziga Vertov
Edited by: Yelizaveta Svilova
Cinematography: Mikhail Kaufman

Synopsis

The Man With the Movie Camera charts a day in the life of a Russian city. We are shown people beginning the day, working through it, and finally relaxing as it draws to a close. Functioning as something of a connecting tissue between these various lives is the 'Man with the Movie Camera' who goes about recording life.

Concept

Dziga Vertov was the Futurist-inspired pseudonym of Denis Abramovich Kaufman. Vertov was apprenticed to Lev Kuleshov who began his career editing news footage and went on to become one of Russian cinema's most vital filmmakers, and the film stands as an example of the Soviet, dubbed, unplayed film; the documentary. Of his identity as a filmmaker, Vertov said, 'I am eye. I am a mechanical eye.'[105] Certainly, this sense of self finds an echo in the closing image of the film and Vertov's guiding principle was to decode reality within a community context, as Graham Roberts discusses in his monograph on the film.

Production

The film was compiled from footage recorded by the Cine Eye production team (Vertov, his brother Mikhail, and Vertov's wife) between 1924 and 1928. As a prelude to embarking on the film, Vertov drafted a manifesto. Indeed, the value of drafting a filmmaking manifesto has endured – we have only to look, for example, to the charter written by the Dogme 95 group. Back to Vertov, though, and an excerpt from the manifesto of August 1922: '…We invite you to flee/the sweet embrace of romance/the poison of the psychological novel…'[106]

Text: Drama, Image, Sound

The statements prefacing the film's first images make clear the self-conscious intentions of the filmmakers; and these intentions, in terms of when the film was made, must surely have been considered shocking in their newness. The opening text reads as follows: 'This film presents an experiment in the cinematic communication of visible events without the aid of intertitles, without the aid of a scenario, without the aid of theatre. This experimental work aims at creating a truly international absolute language of cinema based on its total separation from the language of theatre and literature.'

The film delights in capturing the movement of humans, both individually and in groups, transport and technology. Weaving this together is the titular man with the movie camera as he moves through his world, recording it. The film even contains scenes in which the filmmaker is shown engaged in the process of editing his film. This is not a work that disguises its artifice and craft and, as such, it can be considered honest. Certainly, the film makes a hero of its 'man with the movie camera', and the very first image shows him apparently atop the camera, as though atop a mountain.

The camera is very much a character in this film. In one particular image, we see it in the right foreground of a wide shot looking down on the city, and this emphasises its surveillance qualities.

The film commences with a very self-aware sequence in which we see a strip of celluloid being threaded through a projector, testifying in some degree to the allure film viewing must still have had over so many. The film celebrates the machinery, as much as anything else, prompted by Vertov's political commitment to the cinematic expression of Socialist ideals and policies. The film's prelude concludes with a now-iconic image of a human eye composited over the image of a camera lens: this film is about eye-dentity. In the final minutes of the film, Vertov delights in animation as a movie camera is shown assembling itself and attaching itself to a tripod before walking off of its own volition.

Reception and Legacy

The film was previewed by the Ukrainian Photo and Cinema Administration (VUFKU) in the autumn of 1928 and was first shown publically in Kiev on 8 January, and in Moscow on 9 April 1929. Immediately after the screening, the film's exhibition life halted. *Man With the Movie Camera* was massively influential worldwide, but in Stalinist Russia Vertov soon became outmoded because his wasn't a social-realist approach. The film has been described by film scholar Graham Roberts as 'a document of a period of transition in the history of the Soviet Union, of modernism and Constructivism – indeed of the cinema itself'.[107] By contrast, Paul Rotha, so key to the development and standing of film reviewing, said of the film that 'Vertov was regarded really as rather a joke, you know. All this cutting and one camera photographing another camera – it was all trickery and we didn't take it seriously.'[108]

Contrary to Rotha's view, it would seem that Vertov's film remains relevant and influential on moving-image makers as we view it here in the twenty-first century.

Battleship Potemkin (1925)

Directed by: Sergei Eisenstein
Written by: NF Agadzhanova-Shutko
Edited by: Sergei Eisenstein
Cinematography: Eduard Tisse

Synopsis

The battleship *Potemkin* is at sea. The sailors find their conditions intolerable and rebel. The captains are reluctant to allow the working sailors to express their dissatisfaction and order the mutinous soldiers to be held at gunpoint. The sailors overcome the authorities and news of the mutiny spreads to the port of Odessa. One of the sailors leading the mutiny is killed on the ship and is then rowed to the Odessa shore where the people come and mourn this heroic figure. The uprising captures the imagination of the people and they swarm towards the ship, only for the Tsar's soldiers to confront and kill many of them. The sailors on board the *Potemkin* take the ship out to sea where it fends off attack.

Concept

Sergei Eisenstein saw film as a political device, as a means through which the audience could be mobilised to action. The broader concept was to produce a range of films that would narrate, and move towards the status of myth, the events and people of the Russian Revolution. *Potemkin* dramatises and celebrates the failed 1905 uprising by refracting it through the *Potemkin* event only.

Production

The film's production is perhaps notable for the efficiency with which such a seemingly large-scale endeavour was completed. The *Potemkin* was recreated using two ships: one, the *Twelve Apostles*, had been a sister ship of the *Potemkin*, and a second ship, named the *Komintern*, which was a cruiser, was used as the site for many of the shots and scenes showing the *Potemkin* at its busiest. For the film's climax as the *Potemkin* sails free, the shots of other battleships closing in are taken from existing archive footage of non-Russian naval vessels.

For the recreation of the Cossacks massacring the Russian workers, Eisenstein staged the action on the Odessa Steps, though the event itself had not actually occurred there. To film on the steps, and lend the moment a sense of energy and scale, Eisenstein had a dolly track constructed that ran the length of the steps. Aesthetically, Eisenstein's tracking shot was notable as Russian cinema had tended not to use a mobile camera in this way previously, and several cameras rolled simultaneously on this politically charged action sequence.

The film is justly celebrated for its Odessa Steps sequence, but, ironically, Eisenstein had not designated this as a location in the actual screenplay. Instead, he was 'inspired' to utilise the location by his presence in Odessa. Of this 'epiphany' Eisenstein reflected in his writing that 'I believe that nature, circumstances, the setting at the moment of shooting, and the filmed material itself at the moment of montage, can sometimes be wiser than author and director.'[109]

Text: Drama, Image, Sound

The film has the quality of a tone poem, functioning almost as a series of tableaux that express the idea of uprising in the face of oppression. There are no characters to speak of in terms of highly individual people. Instead there is the presentation of a mass of people. As such, the film plays out like an emblem, a visual song, a series of variations on a theme.

Battleship Potemkin is both war film and political film. It is marked by its accumulation of shots through editing to create motion, kinetic energy and emotion, and to create connections that carry meaning. The film is simultaneously documentary and fiction and the images of the ship's chaplain carry a Biblical power. The film is not subtle in its effects or intent, but it is captivating. Images of masses of people are key to the film's visual content and therefore meaning.

Reception and Legacy

Much has been written about the film which, ultimately, enjoyed far more of a high profile outside of its country of origin. That said when the film was originally screened in France and England it had been done so in private, rather than public screenings. The great Russian poet Vladimir Mayakovsky proclaimed, after seeing the film at its premiere on December 21st 1925, that it should be seen as far and wide as possible. After seeing it, the Hollywood producer, David O Selznick, who went on to produce *Gone With the Wind*, wrote that it was worthy of being seen 'in the same way that a group of artists might study a Rubens or a Raphael... unquestionably one of the greatest motion pictures ever made'.[110]

NATIONAL CINEMA MOVEMENTS

It's an ongoing part of the excitement of cinema that national cinemas rise, fall, reinvent themselves, re-emerge, fuse, and take it in turns to steal the limelight. In this age of home video, DVD and downloading, access to wider film culture has never been easier. Festivals proliferate and there is a genuine enthusiasm and hunger on the part of audiences for films from beyond the world of the mainstream, genre movie. The idea of a 'national' cinema can be considered a construction and film theorist Andrew Higson, in his essay *The Concept of National Cinema*,[111] has discussed it in those terms, writing that we can think about national cinema in terms of economics, subject matter, representation of national character, and how and where the films are shown.

National cinemas that have powerfully announced themselves over the decades include the cinemas of Iran, Australia, Germany, Japan, China, Mexico and India. Furthermore, would it be fair to describe North America's 'national' cinema as the Hollywood studio film; and, if so, how does the issue of the large, industrially organised studio sit within the current filmmaking climate where the producer can also be the distributor via online networks?

Critically, there may not be one definitive national cinema for each territory but instead a number of them.

The films discussed in this section have commonalities and differences, but all were committed to reinvigorating cinema at a given moment in time. Just a small range of national cinemas are considered here as representative of certain movements, and it's fair to say that they could also be considered, for example, in terms of authorship and genre. To some degree the categories are always fluid, but national cinema in terms of subject and style are the key concerns in this section.

FRANCE

Jules et Jim (1961)

Directed by: François Truffaut
Written by: François Truffaut
Produced by: François Truffaut and Marcel Berbert
Edited by: Claudine Bouche
Cinematography: Raoul Coutard
Cast: Jeanne Moreau (Catherine), Oskar Werner (Jules), Henri Serre (Jim), Marie Dubois (Thérèse), Vanna Urbino (Gilberte), Sabine Haudepin (Sabine)

Synopsis

In the early years of the twentieth century, two young men, Jules and Jim, enjoy the good life in Paris. Women are the focus of their lives and, when they meet Catherine, it proves to be a life-changing moment for the three of them. Jules soon falls in love with Catherine as Jim looks on. The First World War begins and Jules and Jim go off to fight. Jules and Catherine marry and live in the Rhone valley in a rural idyll. Jim's literary career takes off and he eventually comes to visit Catherine, Jules and their little girl, Sabine. During his stay, his long-burning passion for Catherine is rekindled and her own unhappiness with her marriage leads to them developing a relationship in full view of Jules. As the years pass, the triangle between Catherine, Jules and Jim becomes increasingly fraught.

Concept

As a key player in the French New Wave of the 1950s, François Truffaut was vocal about his creative debt to directors such as Jean Renoir and Alfred Hitchcock. Renoir represented the 'art cinema' sensibility and Hitchcock the populist approach. If we can imagine a fusion between the approaches of these two filmmakers, it might help us reach an understanding of the range of cinematic devices employed by Truffaut and his similarly 'legendary' contemporaries, most notably Jean-Luc Godard who made such oblique statements as, 'Tracking shots are a question of morality.'[112]

1959 was the watershed year for the French New Wave, with a number of key films released embodying the movement's spirit: *Paris Belongs to Us* (Jacques Rivette, 1960), *A Bout de Souffle* (Jean-Luc Godard, 1960), *Les Cousins* (Claude Chabrol, 1959) and *The 400 Blows* (François Truffaut, 1959). *The 400 Blows* won the Palme d'Or at the Cannes Film Festival. Rather like the Italian neorealist films of the mid- and late-1940s there was an endeavour to make French cinema explore human experience with a certain fidelity to reality.

Godard committed to re-imagining cinema's capacities and challenging audiences. Just watch a film like *Tout Va Bien* (1972) for evidence of this.

It might be fairly accurate to suggest that the French New Wave, like other avant-garde cinema movements, was a conscious effort to provide an alternative to the dominance of the American, studio-produced movie. As such, it's very much an issue of identity. The avant-garde movie is defined as much by what it's about as it is by how it was produced and distributed; and in these days of YouTube and equivalent outlets, the concept is all the more alive and vibrant.

So an art movie isn't only defined by its story, but by the conditions in which it has been produced. There's also been a tendency to emphasise a certain kind of realism, quite in contrast to the artifice of the studio-produced picture. Art cinema, though, is still a product-led process with an economic structure and an audience with expectations that need satisfying. Jean-Luc Godard's *Alphaville* (1965) is an 'art cinema' science-fiction film that embodies many of the traits and tendencies that defined the French avant-garde film movement of the 1950s and 1960s.

In the years immediately following the end of World War Two, France was inundated by a backlog of American movies that had been banned during the conflict. The 1950s, then, became a major moment in the evolution of French cinema and, in part, created the conditions under which the French New Wave movement flourished. The French New Wave, then, was one more link in the chain of refreshing, renewing, re-inventing and making the old new. Jill Forbes has observed that 'the war had brought home film's significance as a means of propaganda and as a way of promoting national cohesion'.[113]

The French New Wave was a conscious movement, in part codified by a 1954 manifesto, *The Time of Contempt: A Certain Tendency of French Cinema*, written by critic, and later filmmaker, François Truffaut, for *Cahiers du Cinema*. Then, too, there were the *francs-tireurs* (the independents). For Truffaut the idea was to create a cinema of authored, identifiable movies. The term *nouvelle vague* was coined by French journalist Françoise Giraud. For the New Wave director, there was a refusal of the 'tradition of quality'. Which means what? Well, the term had originally been used not by Truffaut but by journalist Jean-Pierre Barot in *L'Ecran francais*, and it referred to the assumed middlebrow respectability of French cinema's tendency to adapt literary source material and to do so without much sense of filmic dynamism.

The New Wave blurred lines of difference and distinction between writers, directors and actors. In turn, this mode proved immensely attractive to certain American filmmakers of the late-1960s and 1970s. Perhaps the most accurate observation we can make is that there is an ongoing, unfolding reciprocity of working methods and aesthetic approaches between all the film-producing cultures of the world.

Another defining quality of the French New Wave, espoused by Claude Chabrol, was that small subjects were utterly valid, and this fits somewhat with the literary idea of writing what you know. Jill Forbes again: 'The preoccupations of the *nouvelle vague* matched those of the more clearly avant-garde directors like Alain Resnais or Agnès Varda, whose films explicitly interrogate the relationship between fiction and documentary and between naturalism and formalism. However, it was the sexual politics of *nouvelle vague* films that occasioned most re-evaluation.'[114]

Another filmmaker for whom cinema was a chance to investigate harsh human truths and dilemmas was Robert Bresson whose work includes *Mouchette* (1966), *A Man Escaped* (1956), *Au Hasard Balthazar* (1966), *Pickpocket* (1959), *The Trial of Joan of Arc* (1962) and *L'argent* (1983).

Truffaut's film *Jules et Jim* was adapted from a novel by 75-year-old Henri-Pierre Roché. The film has visual flair. It covers 20 years in the lives of three characters: friends Jules and Jim, and Catherine, the woman they both love. The film is a classic of the French New Wave and, like other French New Wave movies, is steeped in references to other media.

Production

Consistent with the spirit of the New Wave, *Jules et Jim* was filmed on location and built on the example of the Italian neorealist tradition.

Truffaut found the source novel at a second-hand bookstall in Paris in 1955. It was the author's first novel and Truffaut felt confident that it would make the basis of a compelling film. Truffaut spent two weeks in September 1960 at the Colombe d'Or in Saint Paul de Venice rewriting the script as he hadn't liked the draft he had given to Henri-Pierre Roche, the novel's author, in 1957. He used Roché's notebooks to inform the revision. The new draft was much more about Catherine's love for both Jules and Jim.

Jeanne Moreau and Truffaut had a warm working relationship and he felt compelled to cast her in a film in which she could be seen smiling, quite a contrast with her downbeat work in Michelangelo Antonioni's *La Notte* (1961). Accounts of pre-production on *Jules et Jim* all attest to it being a happy experience, though Truffaut, like many filmmakers before and since, was concerned about who would distribute the film. Production began in Normandy on 10 April 1961. The eventual first cut of the film ran to 150 minutes and so needed to be compressed. To enhance the work further, Truffaut called in an ally, a journalist-turned-filmmaker named Jean Aurel, who worked with him on refining the film's structure. Compounding Truffaut's creative anxieties were intense fears about death.

Text: Drama, Image, Sound

One of the great tragic love stories, *Jules et Jim* sees one man struggle to pursue happiness and another quietly resign himself to life's disappointments. The closing image of Jules walking alone along a pathway is heavy with the weight of loss that life brings with it.

The film's music score by Georges Delerue is bittersweet throughout, ably supporting the action and functioning in its own right as a musical entity away from the images. As the relationship between Jules, Jim and Catherine becomes more complicated, so the score becomes less innocent.

Truffaut's debt to Renoir is evidenced in the use of wide shots that bind the protagonists together as they go about their business. · Longer takes also dominate and cuts to close-up are minimal.

By intercutting archive footage in with the new material, the film powerfully contextualises its drama and makes it all the more authentic. Like *La Règle du Jeu*, the film alludes to the rise of fascism; also, despite their fraught personal lives, mutual civility characterises the relationship between Jules and Jim, just as it does that of Chesnaye and Jurieu. It's easy to see why Renoir was such a fan of Truffaut's 'miniature' of the older filmmaker's movie.

The ideal of life and young people's perception of it is underlined – not in the most subtle way, yet neither is it lessened in its resonance – early in the film when Jules and Jim marvel at a stone sculpture of a woman's face with a calm smile. This ideal of womanhood will be what they respond to in Catherine. As Jules and Jim race her across a bridge in an image that is now iconic, a rare close-up, in profile, of Catherine as she runs rhymes with an earlier shot of the carving; and later in the film, as she sits in the chalet, the shot repeats again.

'*Jules et Jim* will be a hymn to life and death, a demonstration through joy and sadness of the impossibility of any love combination apart from the couple,' wrote Truffaut in a letter (now in the archives of Les Films du Carosse) to Helen Scott who ran the French Film Office in New York City on 26 September 1960.[115]

Life's losses and how we must learn to live with them is the great truth of the film. In its own melancholy way, it comforts. Jules comments that 'the disgusting part of war is it deprives a man of his own individual battle.'

Reception and Legacy

Jean Renoir loved the film and wrote to Truffaut: 'It is very important for men to know where we stand with women and equally important for women to know where they stand with men... For this, and for many other reasons, I thank you with all my heart.'[116] Jean Cocteau thought the film caught Roché's work very well and the film generally received positive reviews everywhere.

One review of *Jules et Jim* talks about how the 'film's "rondo of love" represents both a backward glance at the best of the past and a forward glance into cinema's future'.[117]

AUSTRALIA

Picnic at Hanging Rock (1975)

Directed by: Peter Weir
Written by: Cliff Green
Produced by: Hal McElroy and Jim McElroy
Edited by: Max Lemon
Cinematography: Russell Boyd
Cast: Rachel Roberts (Mrs Appleyard), Vivean Gray (Miss McCraw), Helen Morse (Mlle de Poitiers), Kirsty Child (Miss Lumley), Anthony Llewelyn-Jones (Tom)

Synopsis

In 1899, a group of teenage boarding-school girls go for a picnic at Hanging Rock. Their experience in the wilderness proves unsettling and three students and a teacher disappear without any apparent explanation. One of the girls is later found alive but cannot recall what has occurred. The film focuses on the aftermath of the mysterious event and the attempts of various people to understand what has happened.

Concept

Picnic at Hanging Rock is, like other Peter Weir films, infused with images of nature and wilderness. In keeping with other titles that are seen to comprise the Australian New Wave, the film engages with national identity.

The film is based on a story written by Joan Lindsay in 1967. With typical eloquence and thoughtfulness, Peter Weir has described some of the creative choices he made, saying that, 'We worked very hard at creating an hallucinatory, mesmeric rhythm, so that you lost awareness of facts...'[118]

In terms of broader Australian narratives of itself we can understand the film in terms of the relationship between the civilisation of human experience set against, and within the context of, the expanse of wilderness that characterises the Australian interior. Furthermore, there is a tension that has been explored between Australia and its Commonwealth identity. Peter Weir's war film, *Gallipoli* (1981), explores this and Australia's separation after World War One from Great Britain.

Film production in Australia had a long history, though in the 1950s and 1960s the situation changed and the industry barely functioned. To correct this, film funding from government was established with the inauguration of the Australian Film, Television and Radio School. The effect was dramatic and between 1970 and 1985 the Australian film industry produced 400 films. Australian New Wave cinema was a rich and productive moment in time during the 1970s. Paul Cox, John Duigan, Bruce Beresford, Peter Weir, Gillian Armstrong and George Miller all came to prominence in the late 1960s and 1970s. Another wave of filmmakers came to the fore in the early 1990s, notably Baz Luhrmann and Scott Hicks.

Production

In 1970, the Australian government established the Australian Film Development Corporation and this, in turn, facilitated the beginning of a particularly distinct phase in national film production. *Picnic at Hanging Rock* was a major entry in this wave of new filmmaking. The film was shot at the actual Hanging Rock, which is located about 50 kilometres northwest of Melbourne. Stories circulated that the set was haunted.

Text: Drama, Image, Sound

Perhaps to a more overt degree *Picnic at Hanging Rock* fuses the unknowable with the very real. The elements of nature suffuse the film. As with all Peter Weir movies, the original music is supplemented by source music from the classical music world, and, here, Beethoven's 'Emperor Concerto' features. The clash of civilisation and wilderness is accentuated by the décor of the school. There, the girls inhabit a decorous, delicate, fussy world, clearly shown in the opening sequence of the film.

Reception and Legacy

The film was a modest commercial success but has ultimately developed a real following and recognition as a 'classic' of the new Australian cinema of the 1970s. Roger Ebert enthused that here is 'a film of haunting mystery and buried sexual hysteria'.[119] According to *Time Out*, however, 'the atmospherically beautiful images merely entice and divert. The result is little more than a discreetly artistic horror film.'[120]

Weir's film continues to stand tall today as a period drama with a very distinct feeling to it. *The Piano* (1993), directed by New Zealander Jane Campion, connects with Weir's film in terms of images and an overall sensibility that also communicates the clash between the decorous, the civilised and the primal.

GERMANY

Wings of Desire (1987)

Directed by: Wim Wenders
Written by: Peter Handke
Produced by: Anatole Dauman and Wim Wenders
Edited by: Peter Przygodda
Cinematography: Henri Alekan
Cast: Bruno Ganz (Damiel), Solveig Dommartin (Marion), Peter Falk (The Filmstar), Otto Sander (Cassiel), Curt Bois (Homer)

Synopsis

Berlin, 1987. Two angels watch over the inhabitants of the city, interceding in their day-to-day lives. We hear their thoughts as they move through the city observing mortals and doing their best to help and engage with them. In the city, a film is shooting and its Hollywood star is able to see the angels. When one angel falls in love with a trapeze artist and wants to be with her, he renounces his immortality and becomes mortal, wandering the streets of the city, discovering different people as he searches for the woman he loves. His angel friend is pained by this.

Concept

Wings of Desire represents something of an apotheosis for the New German Cinema of the 1970s, which brought to light filmmakers such as Wim Wenders, Werner Herzog, Margarethe von Trotta, Alexander Kluge and Rainer Werner Fassbinder. The New German Cinema was in part defined by a generational sense that there was a need to engage with the national sense of self in the aftermath of World War Two. However, 'unlike Italian neorealism or the French *nouvelle vague*, New German Cinema was not a new style of cinema' and, in the 1970s, German filmmakers were 'uncomfortable with or even suspicious of German films'.[121]

Wenders, like his contemporaries, emerged as a filmmaker at a time when the German government was investing in filmmaking through supportive subsidy schemes. The films being produced had an 'art house' cachet that made them very appealing overseas, which in turn boosted their profile on home ground.

Wenders was born in 1945 and grew up in a Germany that was still an American-occupied nation, with lots of American influence filtering its way into the culture. Putting it in very general terms, American culture colonised Germany in these post-war years.

In movie terms, this meant the powerful examples of Nicholas Ray, Samuel Fuller and John Ford. 'The filmmakers of Wenders's generation, whose film roots were in American cinema, faced certain ambiguities in their attempts to establish a national film culture.'[122] This shot of Americana to the German cinematic psyche gave the German filmmakers of the 1970s a very useful, shared cinematic language. In subsequent years, Wenders's movie muse was Japanese filmmaker Yasujiro Ozu whose work is characterised by a focus on ordinary lives and the tension between stillness and motion.

Of his generation, Wenders perhaps stands as the most 'successful' and was one of the filmmakers synonymous with European cinema in the 1970s and 1980s. Tellingly, Wenders had always practised as a landscape painter, and this eye for place gives great strength to the visual design and scope of *Wings of Desire*.

Wenders has commented that, 'Personally (and hence my problem with stories), I believe more in chaos, in the inexplicable complexity of all those things around me.'[123]

In conceiving a visual design for *Wings of Desire*, Wenders wanted the camera to mimic the point of view of the angels. He was also plagued by the classic dilemma of the creative soul who has too many ideas to pour into the story. The thematic core of the film is that knowledge of self and others is fundamental to our experience of the world and our place in it. The angels in the film become conduits for a range of understandings and for a reflection on Germany's recent past.

Peter Handke wrote a script emphasising poetic dialogue; no full, traditionally written screenplay was produced. Instead, Wenders worked on specific sequences that were inspired and shaped by Handke's written word.

The film is about storylines and the visual design, dominated by long takes, allows the storylines to play out believably and compellingly as we delight in the skill of the illusion making.

In *Wim Wenders: The Logic of Images*, there is a copy of his first treatment for the film, in German, entitled *Der Himmel über Berlin* (The Sky Over Berlin). 'The thing I wished for and saw flashing was a film in and about Berlin… it's the desire of someone who's been away from Germany for a long time and who could only ever experience

"Germanness" in this one city.'[124] Influences on the development of the film's ideas were Rilke's *Duino Elegies*, Paul Klee's paintings and Walter Benjamin's *Angel of History*. There is also a clear debt to Ingmar Bergman and the body of work he produced investigating spiritual crisis.

Production

Wenders began to conceive what would become *Wings of Desire* during his testing time working within the Hollywood system on the film *Hammett* (1982) for Francis Coppola's Zoetrope Studio. In 1985, Wenders returned to Berlin with plans to shoot *Until the End of the World* (1991), but that got delayed. Wenders saw Berlin as a link between the past and the future. Two years after the film was released, the Berlin Wall came down.

Text: Drama, Image, Sound

Wings of Desire is one of cinema's most beautiful films: beautiful to look at, to listen to and to think about after its story is told. The point has been made that one of the key ideas the film communicates is that of rootlessness, of having no home. 'Wenders's films could be analysed exhaustively by their references to borders, and by the various attempts to traverse an inner and outer world...'[125]

In the cinema of Wim Wenders, the theme of identity has often been placed in the context of a fascination with American cinema and the road movie. By contrast, *Wings of Desire* focused on Berlin's divided identity in the 1980s. The film was duly given a follow up, again directed by Wenders, entitled *Faraway, So Close* (1993). In the 1990s, *City of Angels* (1998) was a remake of *Wings of Desire* relocated to Los Angeles.

The film's black-and-white scheme is occasionally intercut with shots and scenes rendered in colour. It is overtly designed but not in a cloddish or clinical way. The design of the angels' costumes is understated and fresh, whilst also communicating the idea that here is a tribe of the afterlife.

The film's dominant compositional approach is built around an almost always gracefully moving mobile camera that elegantly binds characters and situations together, underpinning the idea of the connections between us all. In this way, the style recalls that of filmmaker Theo Angelopoulos whose film *Ulysses Gaze* (1995), for example, functions as a meditation on film as collective memory and the relationship of past to present. This fascination with time embodies itself further in the way the film is constructed around sustained, delicately paced long takes in which the camera moves with slow precision through space, towards characters and then away from them.

Sombre music plays throughout the film, and the 'heartbeat scene' of *Wings of Desire* occurs in a library where we see angels helping people study, read, investigate and contemplate. Wenders has made a compassionate film and that is its great victory.

Peter Falk, playing himself, is shown acting in a World War Two movie that allows the film to engage with Germany's warlike past, and the film occasionally intercuts archive footage of bombed-out Berlin. We see an old man wandering around the wasteland of Potsdamer Platz, sitting in an abandoned chair. The old man is something of the film's conscience, encapsulating its insistence on the importance of remembering and story. When he looks through book of photos in the library, and the film then cuts to archive footage of the dead in Berlin, we understand the film's heartfelt efforts to tie past and present together. 'Where are my heroes?' the old man asks.

Throughout, the film employs the 'pillow-shot' technique so identifiable with Wenders's movie hero Yasujiro Ozu, which David Bordwell defines (in relation to Ozu) as 'empty transitional passages'.[126] There is a meditative power to these images. The film also employs a range of motifs to embody its themes and this approach manifests itself down to the tiniest detail of costume.

The trapeze artist is shown wearing angel-wing earrings at one point. References to other films include the very first image, which shows a brooding sky recalling the opening scene of *The Seventh Seal*. Indeed, *Wings of Desire* has the same openly philosophical attributes as Bergman's film.

The variety of forms of love, passionate and compassionate, that *Wings of Desire* explores manifests itself in a completely charming scene in which Peter Falk and Bruno Ganz talk at a coffee bar. It's rather as if the film is saying that it is the small gestures that count. Early on, Bruno Ganz's character says, 'It's great to live by the spirit,' but this will change for him when he falls in love. After that, he doesn't want to be infinite and eternal.

Touchingly, Wenders dedicates his film to his filmmaker heroes: Yasujiro Ozu, François Truffaut and Andrzej Wajda, all of whom used a sophisticated, understated film style as an expression of their attempts to invigorate cinema with a recognisable human truth.

Reception and Legacy

In the *Washington Post*, Desson Howe wrote playfully that 'Wings perhaps makes the mistake of lingering over its one-note theme, but that note is so lovely, the error – if it is such – is minor'.[127]

USA

It might be sentimental, it might be accurate, but it seems to be a mindset that's lodged firmly in the heads of filmgoers: the 1970s and American cinema were a powerful combination, in effect an American New Wave, producing filmmakers with an acute sense of the powerful attraction of the notion of the film author, as well as an awareness of the tension between individual expression and the commercial demands of the Hollywood studios. It was a time when the American popular cinema experienced a paradigm shift as the studios that had established their identities between the 1920s and 1950s were purchased by corporations and thrown into flux.

There was a sense that the typical kinds of filmmaking were becoming outmoded. As such, there was an opportunity for new filmmakers with a connection to the youth audience to find a foothold. *Easy Rider* (1969) was key to the American New Wave's leaning towards esoteric yet still accessible films, with physical independence from Hollywood being key to this. Central to this effort, arguably leading it, was Francis Coppola, who directed *Rain People* (1969) and thereafter *The Godfather* (1972), and most recently *Tetro* (2010). He has said of the era of the 1970s, when he came to prominence, that 'in any art movement, it's always about four or five artists, you know? Even when you think of Guillermo del Toro and Cuarón and that, they're sort of competing and they're friends, and that was the case for us because we were friends and we liked each other. I think that's a very healthy thing, so I think groups of young people involved in some sort of movement, whether it's political or artistic, or they have an idea like Lars von Trier, they have a concept – Dogme and what have you – those are wonderful youthful expressions. That's why the cinema hops around from country to country – all of a sudden there's a great cinema in Japan, then all of a sudden there's a great cinema in France and England, beautiful films were made especially in that period, in the 1950s post-war. There does seem to be something that makes the cinema hop around the world – and usually it comes from a group of friends who are very much admiring one another but also competitive at the same time.'[128]

Films frequently held up as examples of this era are *The Conversation* (1974), *Badlands* (1973), *Shampoo* (1975), *Bad Company* (1972), *American Graffiti* (1973), *McCabe and Mrs Miller* (1971), *Nashville* (1975), *Taxi Driver* (1976), *Carrie* (1976), *Star Wars* (1977) and *The Sugarland Express* (1974). The period was defined in part by a sense of cultural malaise manifested in the Vietnam War and the Watergate scandal. Ultimately there may be something redundant in defining films by decade. That aside, these films were often characterised by a sense of realism, adopting lessons learnt from the French New Wave and the neorealist movement, and they took the Hollywood mode in a slightly new direction. Even the most generic stories, such as *The French Connection* (1971) or *Jaws* (1975), were rendered with some palpable quality of realism. Even amidst the artifice of these genre movies we could sense the impact on Hollywood storytelling of the general trend towards realism in world cinema.

There was, however, also a place for a more self-conscious poetic mode and a more graphically inclined style, as evidenced by *THX 1138* (1971) and, amongst others, Peter Fonda's film *The Hired Hand* (1971). Of the cinema of the 1970s, it has been commented that the films and filmmakers had new opportunities because anti-trust laws meant that the studios had to break up their producing, distribution and exhibition business model of vertical integration, and, more tangibly perhaps, television had become such a serious challenge to theatrical moviegoing. In turn, studios began banking on a few expensively produced features, such as *Dr Dolittle* (1967). When a film such as *Dr Dolittle* proved a commercial failure, the studio impact was immediate.

As the 1970s witnessed the emergence of new filmmakers it was apparent also that they were finding invigorating ways to make well-established genre movies (horror, action, thriller, adventure, western, science fiction) speak to a new generation of wide-eyed moviegoers for whom some of the myths constructed by 'old' Hollywood remained hugely compelling. I want to use the largely unknown *The Hired Hand* as an example of this approach. It's a beautiful film that is carried, in its own way, by the same ambition that marks much more widely recognised films of the period.

The Hired Hand (1971)

Directed by: Peter Fonda
Written by: Alan Sharp
Produced by: William Hayward

Edited by: Frank Mazzola
Cinematography: Vilmos Zsigmond
Cast: Peter Fonda (Harry), Warren Oates (Arch), Verna Bloom (Hannah), Robert Pratt (Dan), Severn Darden (McVey)

Synopsis

Harry and Archie have been riding for seven years. Harry left his new marriage as he wasn't ready. They now ride with Dan. They arrive in a desert town and Dan is shot dead for going with a woman not knowing she was married. Archie has plans to head for California. Harry has plans to go back to his estranged wife. They go to her farm. Harry and Archie work as hired hands. Gradually Harry and Hannah rekindle their love and marriage. The past returns and Archie is taken prisoner and Harry must go and free him. There is a shootout and Harry dies in Archie's arms. Archie returns to Hannah's.

Concept

In May 2010, the actor John Wayne would have celebrated his 100th birthday. Fascinatingly, Wayne's image as a frontiersman in a range of westerns endures, remaining the definitive way of recalling his career. It also reinforces the importance of the western genre to the construction of American national identity, a process perhaps nowhere more powerfully undertaken than in popular film. With that image of Wayne as the physically imposing figure and tough guy in mind, consider *The Hired Hand*. This elegantly made film represents not only a certain stream of western genre movies but is also emblematic of independently produced popular filmmaking of the 1960s and early-1970s in America. The films from this moment in time are all made in a recognisably popular form, but they are also distinguished by a certain quixotic, non-mainstream sensibility. *The Hired Hand* is a distinct example of a post-classical western that evidences great respect for the genre, as did many other 1970s titles, including *The Outlaw Josey Wales* (1976), *Jeremiah Johnson*

(1972) and *Junior Bonner* (1972). *The Hired Hand* was developed very soon after the success of *Easy Rider* and, by all accounts, the studio seemed to be hoping for an *Easy Rider* 'sequel' set within a western milieu. However, *The Hired Hand* is something other than that. The film's screenplay was penned by the Scottish writer Alan Sharp who also wrote *Ulzana's Raid* (1972). Douglas Pye has written that the western often makes romance a key factor of its narratives, a fact, in the context of the genre, that is not often considered at first glance.[129] The delicacy of the romantic love story throws into contrast all the more powerfully the violence of thought and action that typically defines the other plot and character elements. It's a way of sharpening the relationship between the images and ideas of the wilderness and the garden that inform so much American storytelling.

Genre is an evolving form, a means of classification for audiences and producers. It is a fluid concept, always expanding and often hybridising with other genres. When we think about film genres, we can judge them in two ways: their faithfulness to their own generic traditions and their verisimilitude in terms of 'real' life. Genres comprise semantic and syntactic elements, i.e. visual and structural elements that we can readily identify. Of course, the age-old riddle is to ask: which came first – the film or the genre?

The western is one of the longest-established film genres and André Bazin called it 'the American film par excellence'.[130]

The western has typically been regarded as dramatising and visualising the core idea of the conflict and tensions between the wilderness (as a place, and in terms of lawlessness and antisocial behaviour) and civilisation. The western thrived until the early 1960s and, since then, has 'struggled' to survive. However, there is an understanding that the concepts and forms of the western have now worked their way into other genres such as the action film and the thriller, keeping them current and relevant, albeit in disguised and evolving form.

A further acknowledgement of the western's relevance and resonance finds expression in the following: 'In such a critical climate, the western's positivist and progressive associations can be overlooked, its affecting power and aesthetic achievement slighted.'[130]

Production

With *The Hired Hand*, Peter Fonda wanted to show 'what went down' in 'the real West'.[131] When the film was shown to its studio, Universal, they did not know how to market it as it seemed a world away from *Easy Rider*, the film Fonda had made previously. Like that film, though, *The Hired Hand* would be imbued by a sense of ease with the form and also an authenticity of feeling. As Fonda commented in a retrospective documentary about *The Hired Hand*, 'Nobody ever gallops, except in bad westerns. You just ride.'[132]

The film was shot by Vilmos Zsigmond, who was recommended to Fonda by his original choice, Laszlo Kovacs, who was working on another film at the time. They made the film in New Mexico and built the exterior homestead with interiors and movable walls, all in pursuit of realism and a sense of authenticity. The music for the film was performed by a first-time film composer named Bruce Langhorne, a studio musician known to Fonda. It's the equal of Ry Cooder's work on *Paris, Texas* (1984) and is really beautiful.

Text: Drama, Image, Sound

The Hired Hand is a lyrical film that dwells on moments and metaphor. The green landscape comes to suggest rebirth and, appropriately, the morally barren villains base themselves in a dilapidated desert town. As a western, the film expresses so much, by default almost, about the construction of the American identity. It is an accessible work that sometimes chooses to work in more esoteric ways, and this fusion of approaches characterises a significant number of films from this era.

The film's delicacy comes not only from its characters but also from its use of dissolves and momentary freeze-frames on faces. The opening sequence by the river is something of an overture. The film is marked by quietness and an almost 'art house' film style with a willingness to pause and linger on a moment. Consider the shot of Harry in silhouette, looking out at a brooding evening sky. It's a film that has some qualities in common with the world of filmmaker Terrence Malick. The film's realist feel also stems from its use of the long take, such as in the moment when the camera holds on Archie as he rides off from the farm. It's an image, like so many others in the film, which is suffused with the spirit of Americana and rural life. As such, this is not a cowboy movie, but truly a western. It's a beautiful and thoughtful film.

The Hired Hand is about rejuvenation but wraps this concern up in a tragic mode. The characters all fulfil archetypal roles with Archie as the wise and gentle older man and Harry caught midway between impetuous youth and the wish and need to settle as an adult. Hannah is independent, but her love for Harry has never really died. Witness the expression on her face when she sees Archie returning with just Harry's horse. The camera tracks with elegant slowness around from her face in mid-shot to reveal her view of the riderless horse.

Reception and Legacy

On its first appearance, *The Hired Hand* had a very short theatrical release and was subsequently shown on American television in a much abbreviated version that made barely any narrative sense. Vilmos Zsigmond has honestly noted that one reason the film never found an audience on its original release was that 'it was too much like a European movie'.[133] Some years later, the movie gods ensured justice was done and the film's fortunes began to revive. It was not until the late 1990s, however, that the film was restored to its original form and, in the years since, it has enjoyed a kind of quiet renaissance, which testifies to the energy of the American cinema of the early 1970s to reinvent itself.

JAPAN

Japan could be described as a titan of 'national' cinema in the sense that there is a readily identifiable quality to so many of the films made there. The Japanese cinema is well established. Japanese filmmakers were expected to connect with audiences in a sophisticated way and, as far back as the 1920s, studio head Kido Shiro commented that, 'There are two ways to view humanity... cheerful and gloomy. But the latter will not do. We at Shochiku (studio) prefer to look at life in a warm and hopeful way. To inspire despair in our viewer would be unforgivable. The bottom line is that the basis for film must be salvation.'[134] This overt expression of feeling and spirituality may account in part for the ongoing popularity of certain kinds of anime in the West, in that anime films arguably have space in them for a recognition of life beyond the material and physical. For 250 years, from the end of the sixteenth century, Japan re-established its rule by shogun clan. The culture was isolated from the rest of the world, yet Japanese trade and creative life really developed.

In considering 'classic' Japanese cinema, Donald Richie, one of the major Western historians and commentators on Japanese history and culture, described three particular stylistic approaches in Japanese cinema: piecemeal, calligraphic and pictorialist. The films of Kenji Mizoguchi, famously *The Life of Oharu* (1952), could be said to embody the pictorial approach; Yasujiro Ozu, director of films such as *Tokyo Story* (1953), represents the piecemeal approach, in which sequences are highly 'broken up' into close-ups and mid-shots, with occasional fixed camera 'pillow shots' of typically suburban environments; and Akira Kurosawa demonstrates the calligraphic approach, an elaborate, often highly kinetic style that is emblematic of his approach to story in *Seven Samurai* (1954). Richie also notes that 'Japanese filmmakers borrowed extensively from native popular literature, from the theatre's reworkings of Western narrative principles, and from foreign (particularly American) films' conventions of style and structure'.[135]

One of the connecting tissues in the body of Japanese cinema is an examination of the relationship between the traditional and the modern, and by extension the place of technology and science. Films such as *Rashomon* (1950) and *Seven Samurai* enshrine the samurai past of feudal old Japan. Other films, such as *An Actor's Revenge* (1963) and *The Ring* (1998), both emphasise the importance of the concept of revenge. *Gojira* (1954) and *Ghost in the Shell* (1995) both visualise, in very fantastical, science-fiction terms, the nation's anxieties about technology. In the late 1960s, the Japanese New Wave emerged with titles such as *In the Realm of the Senses* (1976), which were indicative of the desire to craft a new kind of cinema that would work in counterpoint to the 'traditional' cinema of filmmakers such as Akira Kurosawa. Indeed, as referenced in the section about the German film *Wings of Desire*, the director Yasujiro Ozu, who specialised as a studio director in the production of dramas set around the home, many of them examining the pressures and subtle rhythms of family life, was a contemporary of Kurosawa's but produced very different kinds of films. *Tokyo Story* (1953), generally considered to be Ozu's 'masterpiece', though very much indebted it would seem to the Hollywood movie *Make Way For Tomorrow* (1937) explores the anxiety of the post-World War Two generation and that of their parents. This is a tragic film and the focus on family connections resonates across many other Japanese films, such as the more recent *Hana Bi* (1997). Perhaps surprisingly, Ozu's influence can be felt clearly in the modern drama of Wim Wenders's *Wings of Desire*. The movements in national cinema are rarely bound by geography and rapidly become assimilated into other moviemaking contexts.

Seven Samurai (1954)

Directed by: Akira Kurosawa
Written by: Akira Kurosawa, Hideo Oguni and Shinobu Hashimoto
Produced by: Sojiro Motoki
Edited by: Hiroshi Nezu
Cast: Toshiro Mifune (Kikuchiyo), Takashi Shimura (Kambei), Keiko Tsushima (Shino), Yukio Shimazaki (Wife), Kamatari Fujiwara (Farmer Manzo), Daisuke Kato (Shichiroji), Ko Kimura (Katsushiro), Minoru Chiaki (Heihachi), Seiji Miyaguchi (Kyuzo), Yoshio Kosugi (Farmer Mosuke), Bokuzen Hidari (Farmer Yohei), Yoshio Inaba (Gorobei)

Synopsis

An army of bandits raids a peasant village. The distraught villagers discuss what to do and go to the village elder who says they should hire samurai to protect the village. Several of the villagers eventually recruit seven samurai who agree to protect the village not for pay but only for a daily meal. The samurai embed themselves into the culture of the village and train the men to prepare to hold their own when the bandits next attack. The samurai are guided by Kambei, their cool-headed leader; Kikuchiyo, meanwhile, proves to be the most explosive and rebellious of the samurai warriors. Critically, Katsushiro has a relationship with one of the young women in the village, thereby transgressing the samurai code. Inevitably, the bandits eventually return and a large battle to protect the village is fought in heavy rain.

Concept

Film scholar Philip Kemp has written that 'with *Seven Samurai*, Kurosawa… set out to debunk some of the more inflated myths that had attached themselves to the samurai'.[136] *Seven Samurai* is a *jidai-geki* film, a period piece, and represents probably Kurosawa's most well-known type of film. His other *jidai-geki* films include *Yojimbo*

(1961) and *Ran* (1985). He also made contemporary dramas such as *Ikiru* (1952) and *Rhapsody in August* (1991).

In developing *Seven Samurai*, Kurosawa was driven by a desire to make a film that was overtly entertaining. At the same time as he was committed to dramatising the cultural values of old Japan, he also drew on his own fascination with the American films of director John Ford, his westerns particularly, though we shouldn't assume that all Kurosawa did was translate an American story form into a Japanese village setting during the age of the samurai. For Kurosawa, understanding Vincent Van Gogh's sense of composition (honoured in Kurosawa's film *Dreams* [1990]), as well as the work of Shakespeare and certain Russian novelists, was as useful as knowing aspects of film style. For Kurosawa, *Seven Samurai* was, in part, a way of enshrining the values of the samurai class (from which his antecedents hailed), as well as of exploring what drives a sense of community.

Production

Kurosawa's *Seven Samurai* had been an expensive production and, indeed, come the late-1960s, Kurosawa had effectively priced himself out of the more modest budgetary scope of Japanese film production at the time, and so headed for Russia, and eventually to North America and Europe for film financing, prompting a far more intermittent rate of films from the early-1970s until his final film of the mid-1990s. *Seven Samurai*, however, is served on a lavish scale.

Text: Drama, Image, Sound

In the Japanese idiom, realism is often secondary to emotion and, consequently, backgrounds can be used in more expressive ways in order to indicate inner emotional and psychological states.

Kurosawa's film combines a certain kind of realism of presentation with visual flourishes, tied to moments of action, that break away from the desire to capture the ordinary in an understated way. This is the calligraphic approach that David Bordwell has cited, where there is a visual kineticism and physical energy to a sequence. Famously, there is a moment when each of the samurai is shown running and the camera tracks with them and cuts between shots of each.

The film uses close-ups of people's faces to powerful effect, and this contrasts with the wide shots showing the landscape and, in the climax to the film, the rain-soaked battle, which is not accompanied by any dramatic music, only the sound of rain, voices and horses.

The film explores the relationship between individual and community and the need to fight tyranny. As such, it has certain connections with the work of Eisenstein and a film such as *Battleship Potemkin*.

Kurosawa's camera is typically locked off and static, and the dialogue overtly communicates a sense of an order or disorder beyond the control of the human. It's dialogue akin to something in Shakespeare or Greek tragedy. Very early in the film, after the village has been raided by the bandits, one of the villagers says, 'The gods want us to die… our rulers do nothing to protect us.' 'We were born to suffer, it's our fate,' is a comment made by another villager. The samurai give the people their sense of self-worth back, and Kambei, the leader of the samurai, and the eldest, commits to the ideal of helping the weak. The first action we see him perform is to shave off his top knot, to disguise his samurai class and instead resemble a priest, in order to rescue a baby.

There is a real sense of authenticity and sense of place to the drama, and an idea that greatness can be anyone's. Mifune's samurai reveals that he is not of high class but instead the son of a farmer. Mifune's performance is captivating, as is the performance of Takashi Shimura who imbues Kambei with stillness and strength.

Reception and Legacy

Critically, *Seven Samurai*, and by extension Kurosawa, contributed to the growing seriousness with which film was being taken as an art form by the late-1950s and into the 1960s. Thanks to Bergman, Fellini, Godard, Truffaut and Ray, to name just a few, cinema was beginning to be regarded as a form of entertainment that was good, not just as a distraction from, but also as a way of engaging with, the world. The films of these directors were being seen as expressions of national character on film, as well as dynamic embodiments of distinct aesthetic approaches to cinema.

The film has been reviewed as follows: 'It moves quickly because the storytelling is so clear, there are so many sharply defined characters, and the action scenes have a thrilling sweep. Nobody could photograph men in action better than Kurosawa.'[137] And: 'Akira Kurosawa's celebrated film, regarded by many to be the major achievement of Japanese cinema, is an epic that evokes the cultural upheaval brought on by the collapse of Japanese militarism in the sixteenth century.'[138]

MEXICO

Mexican cinema as a national cinema has a tradition that reaches back to the late-nineteenth century. As of this writing, it is enjoying a particular moment of energy and recognition with films that include *Y tu mamá también* (Alfonso Cuarón, 2001), *Amores perros* (Alejandro González Iñárritu, 2000), *21 Grams* (Iñárritu, 2003), *Babel* (Iñárritu, 2006) and *Children of Men* (Cuarón, 2006). Its key directors – Iñárritu, Cuarón, Guillermo del Toro, etc – have gone on to work on projects that have their production centres in the American mainstream cinema, but have found ways to keep the work anchored, in part or whole, in the cultural rhythms and concerns of Mexico.

Pan's Labyrinth (El laberinto del fauno) (2006)

Directed by: Guillermo del Toro
Written by: Guillermo del Toro

Produced by: Guillermo del Toro, Alfonso Cuarón, et al
Edited by: Bernat Vilaplana
Cinematography: Guillermo Navarro
Cast: Ivana Baquero (Ofelia), Maribel Verdú (Mercedes), Sergi López (Captain Vidal), Doug Jones (Faun), Ariadna Gil (Carmen)

Synopsis

It is 1944. A forest in Spain serves as a hideout for Spanish, anti-fascist rebels. They are being hunted down by a sinister soldier, Captain Vidal, who has taken an old mill as his headquarters. He is there with his wife and stepdaughter, Ofelia. Ofelia begins to explore the forest and discovers the route into an underground labyrinth where she is met by the faun of the film's title. The faun charges Ofelia with three quests that relate to a larger, fantastical narrative. Ofelia undertakes each challenge and these adventures are woven into the story of the Captain seeking to rout the anti-fascist rebels in the forest. Ofelia's friend, the housekeeper Mercedes, is an ally of the guerrillas.

Concept

Pan's Labyrinth, though set in Spain, exhibits strong traces of its makers' Mexican origins and, in terms of its director, the influence of Catholic image making and the fusion of popular forms of expression and the aesthetics of Mexican murals. Mexican cinema experienced its own new wave in the early-1990s with film such as *Como Agua Para Chocolate* (1992) and *Cronos* (1993). Another factor in the enrichment of Mexican cinema has been an active level of government support via the Mexican Film Institute (Mexicana de Cinematografia) and the evolution of two major film schools. A final key element has been the ways in which the filmmakers who emerged during the 1990s were able to secure creative control over their films. However, because the Mexican government are no longer able to be the only producers of a given film, Mexican filmmakers have been compelled to look internationally for financing. Another feature of 1990s Mexican cinema was the number of women filmmakers who have come to prominence: Busi Cortes, Guita Schyfter, Dana Rotberg and Marisa Sistach.

Pan's Labyrinth functions somewhat as a parable and, for del Toro, it was a chance to explore his own fascination with violence and the choice to be or not be violent. By his own admission, del Toro is a fairytale enthusiast and the film serves as a kind of compendium of approaches to a genre with its own rich cinematic history. Del Toro is aware of the violence inherent in fairytales and the concept for *Pan's Labyrinth* bears this out. In a piece he wrote to promote the release of the film in the UK in late 2006, he commented that, 'To have a fairytale logic but not in a sanitised way, not in a clean, nice sort of child's story, but a much more rough-edged type of illustration or painting, I thought of Arthur Hughes, who had a very perverse sense of design in the Victorian illustration of fables that he did.'[139] The film succeeds as a fantasy film not based on an existing text, which demonstrates the legitimacy of the genre as one that is distinct from science fiction and horror.

Production

Pan's Labyrinth was produced during the first few years of the twenty-first century when Mexico and its filmmakers were at the forefront of world cinema. Iñárritu and del Toro are two of the highest-profile filmmakers whose work engages with preoccupations of Mexican culture and imagination. Iñárritu has commented that what makes Mexican cinema distinct is that 'our films are more concerned with the visceral side of life and not the money side, and we shoot from the pelvis and not from the intellect'.[140]

Del Toro had been approached to direct an adaptation of one of the Harry Potter novels but decided to remain with his *Pan's Labyrinth* project. He has had to raise financing repeatedly outside of Mexico but the films he directs remain determinedly Mexican in certain ways, and their investment in the fantastical and the liminal space between 'reality' and 'fantasy' seems central to this. As his work has broadened in its appeal and in its production circumstances, del Toro has maintained key Mexican collaborators.

In creating the fantasy settings and characters of the film, del Toro did not shy away from computer-generated elements. He has commented that 'there is a very delicate sense of balance in the design of the piece: textures, shapes, colours that articulate the movie in order to sustain the fable in a juxtaposition with the real world'.[141]

Text: Drama, Image, Sound

Pan's Labyrinth fascinates for its fusion of generic impulses, and Mark Kermode has described del Toro as 'the finest living exponent of fabulist film'.[142] Whilst the film's advertising campaign emphasised the fantasy trappings of the story, this writer's immediate reaction to seeing the film was that it was a war film with a fantastical subplot. Del Toro said in *Sight and Sound* in December 2006 that 'a maze is a place where you get lost but a labyrinth is essentially a place of transit: an ethical, moral transit to one inevitable centre'.[143]

The film is so meticulously designed that even the motif on the headboard of the bed in which Ofelia and her mother sleep echoes the image of the faun's face. In this film, the world of the fantastical and numinous is right there next to our world of tangible surfaces. It is a hymn to the need for fantasy in our real, sometimes pained lives.

The film is defined by cold, nightly blues and greens for the subterranean world of the faun. There are also colour schemes built around golds and yellows, and Ofelia's coat in the opening sequence immediately connects her to the greens and browns of the forest world.

The film explores choices made either to give life or sustain a reign of death. The Captain grips and nearly crushes Ofelia's hand early in the film and, throughout, she is associated with life. There are images that linger such as Ofelia's clothes hanging on the branch of the twisted, shattered tree through which she enters the Underground Realm. As the clothes hang, their flax drifts and swirls around.

Del Toro's film luxuriates in its illusion-making and, in this age of digital effects, makes the effective and affecting choice for its title character to be rendered as a live-action performance (by Doug Jones) from beneath an intricate and mesmerising costume and facial make-up.

The film's opening image, which reveals a forest and momentarily a fairy resting on a stone in the foreground, evokes Miyazaki's *Spirited Away* (2001).

The film does not shirk from a number of explicit depictions of violence, and menace underpins the film so that it powerfully obeys the rules of the fairytale mode whereby light and shadow are shown to necessarily co-exist.

Reception and Legacy

When the film was released in 2006, it was greeted enthusiastically as a fantasy film for adult audiences. Typically, critics around the world celebrated the film's intelligence and imagination with observations such as this from the film magazine *Empire*: 'While there are trips into magical worlds, including a memorable encounter with a Clive-Barkerian spectre called the Pale Man which has loose folds of skin and eyeballs in its hands, Ofelia's magical experiences don't overwhelm the film.'[144]

By contrast, there was a more cool-headed note struck by Peter Bradshaw in the *Guardian*: 'What do these creatures say about fascism? Or, what does fascism say about them? It's a bold and intriguing proposition but I'm not sure it comes off.'[145] And *Variety* described it as 'a fairytale not even remotely intended for children'.[146]

DIGITAL CINEMA:
NEW WAYS OF MOVING THE WORLD

It may already be redundant to talk about digital technology as it has now settled into the culture as the norm. That said, the term 'digital' still suggests a technology that is relatively affordable and accessible, resulting in a broadening of the range and diversity of content being produced. It has certainly meant that quieter creative voices have been able to find their place. Digital filmmaking equipment, then, is cheaper, more obtainable and relatively easy to use, and we can make a useful connection between the freedoms allowed by ever-cheaper, increasingly portable technology and that celebrated 'movie movement' moment in time in the late-1950s and early-1960s when filmmaking took to the streets, liberating cinema from a dependency on studio-based production. What would someone like Alexandre Astruc, with his concept of the camera as pen, make of the movies now being made using iPhones and DSLR cameras, and other variations, in the second decade of the twenty-first century?

With acute foresight, filmmaker Francis Coppola, back in the early-1980s, talked about how electronic cinema would someday become a staple of moving-image production. Coppola utilised the early forms of the process when preparing for filming on his two beautifully realised films *The Outsiders* (1983) and *Rumble Fish* (1983), and, more recently, he has continued in the same vein with a pair of small, quixotic projects: the philosophical and melancholy *Youth Without Youth* (2007), and *Tetro* (2009), a story about brothers.

The integration of the computer into filmmaking 40 years ago initiated the long and fascinating walk towards the digital-moviemaking age which has now become the norm. As with colour and sound, the possibilities and limitations of the new technology have, of course, impacted on the creative process.

The term 'digital cinema' can refer specifically to the means used to capture footage, such as a mini DV camera or HD camera. A key film in establishing the viability and particular stylistic forms of digital video was *Russian Ark* (2002) which was filmed in one take at the Hermitage Museum in St Petersburg in Russia. The film utilised 2,000 actors and extras and was filmed after many months of planning and rehearsal. Alternatively, when we think of digital cinema, we might also think of the creation of animated and synthetic elements composited into an existing image. Perfect examples of this are the dinosaurs in *Jurassic Park* (1993), the *Spiderman* (2002–7) films, and the new mode of performance capture. Digital cinema can either refer to shooting on digital, or to using digital technology to create specific elements and painted images in films like *The Polar Express* (2004), *Avatar* (2009) and the Robert Zemeckis film *A Christmas Carol* (2009). The concept of film as painted image provides fascinating opportunities way beyond the narrative feature-film format.

The past ten years have seen an increase in the number of micro-budget filmmakers, and filmmaking work with diverse communities has also flourished with organisations such as the Rural Media Company and Hi8Us working regionally and nationally in the UK. Micro-budget, feature-length films are also being produced and distributed as DVD titles, though some short films continue to be produced on film. Digital cinema is a product of the information age rather than the mechanical age and has caused a paradigm shift across the board, impacting on major studios as well as community-media production companies. The modern-day equivalents of the politically inspired British community arts and media movements of the 1970s have been provided plentiful opportunities for work, and the development of digital production and distribution resources has frequently allowed for far more accurate and telling representations of British experience than the mainstream mode can offer.

Cinema always has, and always will, develop new technologies to augment and evolve what has come before. In the 1980s, Coppola effectively predicted YouTube.

Jean-Pierre Geuens writes that digital image-making is questionable as it seems to suggest that there is 'a deep distrust of the everyday world, the sense that the real stuff is no longer good enough to do the job that is now envisioned for cinema'.[147] In *The Cinema Book* we read that '(the) over-determination of the spectacularly artificial image became the staple of much of Hollywood's late-1980s and 1990s product'.[148]

However, digital-capturing technology has allowed the *vérité* stylings to continue, and for certain stories to be told in more realistic ways, *Atanarjuat* (2001) being a powerful testament to this. Real time, long takes, a sense of real rhythm: all these are akin to the impulse of the Italian neorealist movement.

The digital movie camera really has become the *caméra-stylo* of Alexandre Astruc's understandings and hopes. There are powerful and relevant questions to ask, then, about the benefits and deficits of film and digital. What has been lost in the evolution of digital? What has been gained? Filmmaker Patrick Keiller has written, 'Film tends to involve a greater commitment to an image (than digital video)… This hybridity of photographic and digital media so emphasises the value of the material, mineral characteristics of film that one begins to reimagine cinematography as a variety of stone carving.'[149]

The filmmaker Ingmar Bergman commented about film in the context of the digital age that 'old-fashioned film lighting was really wonderful. It was slightly erotic to have that circle of light – there was magic to it'.[150]

In 2007 and 2009, Francis Coppola directed two films shot on digital video, made with small budgets, which allowed the films a freedom in terms of the range of ideas they grappled with through the drama. The images of *Youth Without Youth* include layerings of material (matching the beautiful efforts to create a layered and meaningfully dense story) and the film was edited in Final Cut Pro. For *Tetro*, green-screen techniques were used for the Powell-and-Pressburger-inflected dance sequence. For the film's editor, Walter Murch: 'There was the issue of keeping a lid on the metaphysics that the novella is crammed with. There were so many plot lines – more than in the final version of the film – and the metaphysical discussions were longer and more intense, so it was a question of finding the right degree of scaling back while still allowing the film to be true to itself.'[151]

Atanarjuat: The Fast Runner (2001)

Directed by: Zacharias Kunuk
Written by: Paul Apak Angilirq
Produced by: Paul Apak Angilirq
Edited by: Norman Cohn, Zacharias Kunuk and Marie-Christine Sarda
Cinematographer: Norman Cohn
Cast: Natar Ungalaaq, Sylvia Ivalu, Peter Henry Arnatsiaq, Lucy Tulugarjuk, Madeline Ivalu

Synopsis

Atanarjuat is based on an existing Inuit tale about a moment in time when a community is besieged by the negative energy and force of a shaman. Tensions overflow and two brothers (Amaqjuaq and Atanarjuat) find themselves challenged by a local gang. Where Amaqjuaq is strong and burly, Atanarjuat is slender and fast on his feet. When the gang kill his brother in a clash of egos, Atanarjuat goes on the run, pursued by the murderers. Atanarjuat endures the harsh Arctic landscape and eventually makes his journey home.

Concept

Zacharias Kunuk, the film's director, has said that '*Atanarjuat* is a universal story with emotions people all over the world can understand. It is also totally Inuit: a story we all heard as children, told and acted by Inuit. We show how Inuit lived hundreds of years ago and what their problems were, starting with their marriage problems... This is the story we are passing on to others, just like it was passed on to us.'[152]

Across the span of film history there have always been films that run counter to the Hollywood mainstream mode, both formally and contextually. The cinemas of diversity possess a willingness to be political and to engage explicitly with the specific concerns of a given culture.

Atanarjuat evidences the relationship between digital technology and realism and marginalised cultures. Again, the spirit of André Bazin hovers over our responses to cinema as it continues to evolve.

Production

The production of *Atanarjuat* represented a major shift upwards in scale and also the culmination of some years' effort in fostering an authentic local and regional production identity – a thing to be celebrated. Zacharias Kunuk is of the first generation of Inuits to read, write and make films. Kunuk and others worked as a collective, with digital technology and access to it playing a major part in allowing this to develop.

Around the world there exists a vibrant video-workshop and community-filmmaking strata that has emerged over the past 40 years or so and which was particularly strong in Britain in the 1970s. This community work, supported by various funding and trust agencies, has created a range of cultural media production centring on subjects mainstream broadcasting and filmmaking do not readily engage with. As such, a wider range of people have found ways of narrating their stories, and watching this film alongside Flaherty's *Nanook of the North* is fascinating.

In making the film, the producers recorded eight elders telling variations on the story of the legend of Atanarjuat. Subsequently, the film's treatment drew these differing stories together into a coherent whole.

Local people were trained by professional filmmakers and this model is something that has currency around the world. Certainly, in the UK, organisations such as the Rural Media Company and Hi8Us have been working in this mode, scoring a great creative success that has resonated in the heartland and at grassroots levels.

Atanarjuat was recorded on digibeta tape and then transferred to film, thereby allowing it a chance of relatively wide theatrical distribution.

In 1983, the Inuit Broadcasting Corporation (IBC) had been established in Igloolik and was run by one man, Paul Apak. The following year, Zacharias Kunuk joined the operation and, over time, they created Igloolik Isuma Productions, Canada's first Inuit independent production company.

Kunuk's early video-making experiences dealt with marginal communities and studies with children. From this starting point he moved into a form of documentary filmmaking and committed himself to the notion of moving images that captured reality rather than transforming it.

Atanarjuat was produced on a budget of US$1.31 million (1.96 million Canadian dollars) and was shot on Igloolik, a small island of 1,200 people in the north Baffin region of the Canadian Arctic. Human culture has been part of the region for 4,000 years.

As a culture, the Inuits have been widely regarded as excelling not at combat, or science, or engineering, but instead at the beautiful and essential act of storytelling. Zacharias Kunuk described his debut feature as 'one way of bringing back lost traditions. I have never witnessed shamanism. I have only heard about it. One way of making it visible is to film it.' The film's director of photography Norman Cohn has noted that 'conventional filmmaking has a hierarchy like the military. Every relationship is vertical, every individual knows exactly who is one notch ahead of him or her or one notch below. Inuit aren't like that. Nobody ever salutes. Inuit process is very horizontal.'

The film aims to immerse its audience in the environment and employs a documentary aesthetic to do so, with its implied, though easily challenged, claim to truth and accuracy.

Atanarjuat, then, showcased an aesthetic that was the summation of smaller TV projects attempting a form of 're-lived drama'. One outcome of *Atanarjuat*'s global success was the creation of Isuma TV, which has gone on to function as an online presence for Inuit filmmaking.

We are therefore at the thrilling moment when access to technology has allowed a range of marginal voices to come forward to express themselves through cinema, and there are funding structures in place to facilitate the production of films that encourage audiences to negotiate and understand the world's diversity. Now more than ever, perhaps, when we say 'film', we do not automatically default to the Hollywood mode.

Text: Drama, Image, Sound

Atanarjuat is an adventure film that foregrounds its mythic antecedents, yet also couches this kind of narrative in a visual treatment more redolent of a so-called 'fly on the wall' documentary. The film revels in being able to depict and re-enact customs, patterns and rhythms of the Inuit culture. Interestingly, the film sits in powerful contrast to a studio movie directed by Nicholas Ray called *The Savage Innocents* (1960). That film was also about Eskimo culture, but its artifice, which would once have claimed to be 'realistic', now looks overwhelmingly ersatz.

In her book *The Idea of North*, Sherril E Grace writes that: 'North is a function of a complex interaction between the colonising imposition of southern and western towns, assumptions, technologies and institutions and the increasing capacity of northerners to appropriate these mechanisms and regimes of power in order to "write back."[153]

Atanarjuat stands in fascinating contrast with Robert Flaherty's documentary, *Nanook of the North*. The more recent film has the quality of a documentary in its pacing and its capacity to dwell on the details of apparently mundane tasks (such as the preparation of a sled) so that they begin to assume their true significance. Shooting the film on video allows for these relatively inexpensive long takes. The film captures the emptiness of the snowy desert, and the use of locked-off, static, wide shots places the people as tiny, fragile specks in their environment. The film moves fluidly between a documentary tone and more direct dramatic moments, but even then the artifice is minimal. There is a sense of this as a family saga and the community's responsibility for its own welfare is critical. The film also indicates that domestic ups and downs are as ordinary a part of Inuit life as any other, and so the exoticism of the setting is kept at bay. The film moves from being a neorealist drama recreating aspects of a specific milieu into a chase film, an adventure.

Atanarjuat, then, underscores the place of regional filmmaking and, very specifically, the film fostered the kind of approach evidenced in the British film *Seadch: The Inaccessible Pinnacle* (Simon Miller, 2007). Indeed, as of this writing, there appears to be a sense that regionally specific filmmaking is important to film-funding agencies in Britain. *Seadch* meditates wonderfully on tradition and the influence of the past on the imagination of the present moment. It's about how a very specific sense of place and heritage can be used to empower.

We live at a moment when seeking to understand our relationship to the wilderness and the past exerts great power over our imaginations and *Seachd* soars with its visual simplicity and elegance; its narrative, sounds and images all reinforce how we are part of the land and how a story forms the bedrock of a person and a place. Aonghas is a boy whose parents have recently died and so he goes to live with his grandparents. As he begins to reconcile himself to the tragedy, Aonghas is enchanted by his grandfather's stories of the past. Dialogue in *Seachd* is spoken entirely in Gaelic. Alternating elegantly composed domestic scenes with wide vistas of the hard and rugged Skye landscape, the film recalls the movies of Lynne Ramsey and Terrence Malick and perhaps also *The Secret of Roan Inish* (John Sayles, 1997). It is an artful expression of real regional filmmaking and its moving climax reminds the viewer of the power of story to heal and nurture.

The philosopher Martin Heidegger has observed that 'technology is no mere means' but 'a way of revealing' and understanding the world, and this arguably takes us back to where this book began, with cinema's display of faith in reality, in the allure of, and the need to replicate, the 'real' world. The perceived downside to all this is posited by Jean-Pierre Geuens when he writes that, 'By radically simplifying the nature of the shooting process, by bringing transparency to it, digital technology pensions off [the] heroic features of film. The image for one is there from the start [as a signal]. It doesn't have to be imagined, produced, begged for, cajoled into existence.'[154] With digital moviemaking, Geuens suggests that we have arrived at a moment in time where a culture driven by the fast and the instantaneous deprives us of being attuned to subtle calibrations.

Reception and Legacy

Atanarjuat: The Fast Runner was well received when released in 2001 and it won awards at film festivals such as San Diego and Toronto in the category of Best Feature. It also won the Camera d'Or at Cannes and in New York's *Village Voice* was described as being 'so devoid of stereotype and cosmic in its vision it could suggest the rebirth of cinema'.[155] This enthusiasm was echoed by a comment in the magazine *Sight and Sound*, which described the film thus: 'Spellbinding as storytelling, it also prompts admiration for the Inuit people's patience, resilience, and their overriding concern for harmony with the world around them.'[156] The publication went on to say that *Atanarjuat* was 'perhaps the purest, freshest burst of mythic narrative that cinema has produced in recent years'.[157]

Waking Life (2001)

Directed by: Richard Linklater
Written by: Richard Linklater
Produced by: Tommy Pallotta, Jonah Smith, Anne Walker-McBay, Palmer West
Edited by: Sandra Adair
Cinematography: Richard Linklater and Tommy Pallotta
Cast: Wiley Wiggins, Julie Delpy, Ethan Hawke, Robert C Solomon

Synopsis

It's a fair bet that Henry David Thoreau would have liked *Waking Life* a fair bit. The movie takes a sauntering young man named Wiley Wiggins and charts his encounters with a rich variety of thinkers and 'evangelists' of thought. The movie concerns itself with a long and rambling lucid dream and Wiley's story is prefigured by a prologue that shows him as a kid playing a paper puzzle game that concludes with the comment: 'Dream is destiny.' The beautiful, airy film in fact feels like a dream. The movie has the quality of a poem, bathed in the Texas sunshine. 'In motion to the ocean' is a worthy creed to grab from the movie and hold close to your heart.

Concept

Waking Life is not tied to the urgent narrative form of most Hollywood films. Instead, the aim is to wilfully refuse the lean, mean and very effective and compelling Hollywood format and instead give the audience a story that loafs along as the young man Wiley Wiggins walks around his hometown, talking and reflecting on both the moment at hand and bigger concerns. This is a glorious stream-of-consciousness film.

Production

Coming to the foreground of the American independent movie scene just before much of that independence was bought up by major American studios in the mid-1990s, director Richard Linklater might be usefully defined as a regional American filmmaker, at least in terms of his earlier work and its Texan settings. With *Slacker* (1991) and *Dazed and Confused* (1993), both live-action movies, Linklater established a very talky aesthetic of rich characters and a surfeit of ideas. His career has been marked by an eclectic range of films (including period drama *The Newton Boys* [1998] and, much more recently, his terrific kids' film, *School of Rock* [2003]). With *Waking Life*, Linklater again played with audience expectations and found a new and arresting way of making vivid his love of dialogue cascading with wit, warmth and reflection.

Linklater had almost given up on turning his script into a movie until he saw the work of Bob Sabiston and Tommy Pallotta who had created the short animated movies *Roadhead* (1999), *Snack and Drink* (2000) and *Figures of Speech* (2000). In a forward-looking throwback, Sabiston and Pallotta essentially used a form of rotoscoping, painting over live-action footage of human movement (a technique that has been used since the earliest days of animation). Instead of using ink and paint, Sabiston uses a paint-like, digital effect which gives to the digitally shot, live-action footage a wonderful, often dislocated floating effect. Linklater applied the same technique to *Waking Life*. It makes the action all the more real, all the more lucid.

A different animator was assigned to each character, creating a real consistency. Of course, in the purest sense, the film is only animated in part, being more of a fusion between live action and the animated format. If you like the leaps and bounds of Jack

Kerouac's freewheeling prose, you might well delight in *Waking Life*. Thoughtful, smart, flip and funny, it feels almost like a very long song. Music plays its part – usually quite mournfully. Certain moments feel like drama, others far more like documentary. *Waking Life* is a film about the small moments that yield the big thoughts. It's a digital epiphany. Linklater has observed that 'this film uses dreams as a kind of operating system for the narrative, the hitch for most of the ideas. The realities of [live-action] film would have cancelled out the ideas.'[158]

Text: Drama, Sound, Image

Waking Life is a beautiful film in which the animated format only makes clearer and more emotionally real the cascade of thought often very humorously presented. This is a free-association kind of movie, a series of riffs on ideas of perception and the sense of the individual in pursuit of worth. The film's style is its content. It depicts a dream state and, in doing so, attains this quality itself. Existentialism, language, belonging, connections: all comprise streams of thought. Animation creates a contract with its audiences where the agreement is a willingness to create and view without limitation or constraint. In the best way possible, anything goes. Flip-flopping between the humorous and the more intense (such as the guy who fills the petrol can), the film ebbs and flows, taking in the highs and lows of existence. This is a lyrical movie about the essentials of living and feeling and perceiving – all rendered with bubblegum elasticity and energy.

Reception and Legacy

Waking Life was reviewed by *Variety* as follows: 'The eagerness and earnestness with which the picture addresses its subjects, and the lack of cynicism with which it does so, is something most people don't necessarily encounter in life after college.'[159]

Monster House (Gil Kenan, 2006), *Beowulf* (Robert Zemeckis, 2007), *Avatar* (James Cameron, 2009) and the forthcoming *The Adventures of Tintin: Secret of the Unicorn* (Steven Spielberg, 2011) are all further iterations of the painterly example set by *Waking Life*.

As has always been the case, it will be fascinating to see how this kind of visual novelty and spectacle fuses with narrative. Indeed, things often get exciting when a 'new' approach becomes 'old hat' and can settle into using form and content together. The 'painterly' is what defines this process of motion and performance capture. The image may contain elements that are animated but, effectively, this is a fascinating new mode of digital imaging that, at the very highest level of technological sophistication, evolves the old tradition of rotoscoping, which we can regard as a kind of puppetry to some degree. The more things change, the more they stay the same.

Beowulf adopts a painterly realism and one of the strengths of the film is its imagination of an environment, and its attention to detailing a culture. Zemeckis's follow-up film, *A Christmas Carol* (2009), evidenced a welcome willingness not to entirely embrace a sense of photorealism, but instead a visual style with something of the mystery, shadow and wonder of the British illustrator Arthur Rackham. In late 2010, Aardman Animation released a short film produced on an iPhone.

We live at a time when the rules of film as photography are beginning to shift. You could say that a watershed moment has arrived (again), which, perhaps most significantly, will broaden access to the production and distribution base for filmmaking. With digital video production and online exhibition increasing, filmmaking tools are in the hands of an ever-broadening demographic, though there is still space for one-off short films shot on Vista Vision cameras such as *Chasing Cotards*.

A widening, ever-varying range of movie movements will come to pass and we can be there to enjoy them all and, as always, have our view of the world and of ourselves broadened and enriched.

Filmmaking now is more of, and for, the people than ever before. Our hearts and minds will never tire of being moved to thought, feeling and action.

In discussing the compelling allure of cinema, Stanley Cavell has written that 'to be human is to wish, and in particular to wish for a completer identity than one has so far attained; and that such a wish may project a complete world opposed to the world one so far shares with others'.[160]

As I finished my work on this book I had a very clear sense of how beautiful film can be, especially its intensity of invention in reminding us of the fascination to be found in telling our stories.

FURTHER READING

Austin, Thomas, *Watching the World: Screen Documentary and Audiences*, Manchester University Press, 2007

Barr, Charles (ed), *All Our Yesterdays*, BFI, London, 1990

Bazin, André, *What Is Cinema, Volume 1*, University of California Press, 2005

Bordwell, David and Thompson, Kristin, *Film Art: An Introduction*, Ninth Edition, McGraw Hill, 2010

Boyd, Brian, *The Origin of Stories: Evolution, Cognition and Fiction*, Belknap Press, 2009

Braudy, Leo and Cohen, Marshall, *Film Theory and Criticism*, Eighth Edition, Oxford University Press, 2009

Bruzzi, Stella, *New Documentary: A Critical Introduction*, Routledge, 2000

Butler, Andrew, *Fantasy Cinema: Impossible Worlds on Screen*, Wallflower Press, 2009

Cavell, Stanley, *Cavell On Film*, edited by William Rothman, State University of New York Press, 2005

Charity, Tom et al, *The Rough Guide to Film*, Penguin Books, London, 2007

Clarke, James, *Animated Films*, Virgin Books, Second Edition, London, 2006

Cook, Pam, *The Cinema Book*, BFI, London, 2008

Cousins, Mark and Kevin McDonald, *Imagining Reality: The Faber Book of Documentary*, Faber and Faber, Revised Edition, 2006

Dabashi, Hamid, *Close Up – Iranian Cinema: Past, Present and Future*, Verso Books, 2001

Donohue, Walter, *Projections series*, Faber and Faber, 1993–2008

Gombrich, EH, *Art and Illusion: A Study in the Psychology of Pictorial Representation*, Sixth Edition, Phaidon, 2002

Grant, Barry Keith and Sloniowski, J (eds), *Documenting the Documentary: Close Reading of Documentary Film and Video*, Wayne State University Press, 1998

Hayward, Susan, *French National Cinema*, Routledge, 1992

Hayward, Susan, *Key Concepts: Cinema Studies*, Routledge, 2006

Kitses, Jim, *Horizons West: Directing the Western from John Ford to Clint Eastwood*, BFI, 2004

Lawton, Anna, *The Red Screen: Politics, Society, Art in Soviet Cinema*, Routledge, 1992

Leyda, Jay, *Kino: A History of the Russian and Soviet Film*, Princeton University Press, 1983

Long, Samantha, *British Social Realism: From Documentary to Brit Grit*, Wallflower Press, 2008

Manvell, Roger, *Cinema*, Penguin Books, London, 1950

Murch, Walter, *In the Blink of an Eye*, Silman James Press, 2001

Murphy, Robert, *The British Cinema Book*, Second Edition, BFI, London, 2003

Nelmes, Jill, *Introduction to Film Studies*, Routledge, Second Edition, 1999

Jill Nelmes, *Cinema and Cultural Modernity*, Open University Press, 2000

Nichols, Bill, *Movies and Methods, Volumes 1 and 2*, University of California, 1985

Ondaatje, Michael and Murch, Walter, *The Conversations: Walter Murch and the Art of Editing Film*, Bloomsbury, 2004

Patterson, Cullen, Allon (eds), *The Wallflower Press Critical Guide to British and Irish Film Directors*

Patterson, Cullen, Allon (eds), *The Wallflower Press Critical Guide to North American Film Directors*, Wallflower Press, 2001

Perkins VF, *The Magnificent Ambersons*, BFI, London, 1999

Perkins, VF, *Film as Film*, Da Capo Press, 1993

Renoir, Jean, *My Life and My Films*, Da Capo Press, 1974

Richie, Donald, *A Hundred Years of Japanese Film: A Concise History*, Kodansha International, Tokyo, 2001

Wells, Paul, *Understanding Animation*, Routledge, 1998

Wenders, Wim, *On Film*, Faber and Faber, 2001

JOURNALS

Cahiers du Cinéma

Cineaste

Electric Sheep

Film Comment

Film Quarterly

Filmint.nu

Filmmaker

Films and Festivals

Imagine

Jump Cut

Little White Lies

Moviescope

Screen

Screen International

Sight and Sound

ONLINE

www.sensesofcinema.com

one of your first stops for information about directors and current debates in the study and enjoyment of cinema

www.bfi.org.uk
the website of the British Film Institute

www.brightlightsfilm.com
the website of film journal *Brightlights*

www.cartoonbrew.com
one of the major animation industry and animation culture websites

www.davidbordwell.net
the website for one of the major film scholars

www.ejumpcut.org
the website for *JumpCut* film journal

www.filmcomment.com
the website for long established American magazine *Film Comment*

www.filmstudiesforfree.blogspot.com
a stunningly wide-ranging blog

www.popmatters.com
a website committed to intelligent discussion of popular culture

www.rouge.com.au
an academic online film journal

www.scope.nottingham.ac.uk
film studies journal published by the University of Nottingham

ENDNOTES

1 Jean-Luc Godard, quoted by Jim Emerson, www.blogs-suntimes.com/scanners/2010/02/the_morality_of_deep_focus_and.html

2 Jim Kitses, *Horizons West: Directing the Western from John Ford to Clint Eastwood*, BFI, 2004, pp.21–2

3 André Bazin, quoted by David Forgacs, *Rome Open City*, BFI, 2000, p.23

4 Jean-Luc Godard, quoted by Douglas Morrey, *French Film Directors: Jean-Luc Godard*, Manchester University Press, 2005, p.173

5 Brian Boyd, *On the Origin of Stories: Evolution, Cognition and Fiction*, Belknap Press: Harvard, 2009, p.95

6 Jean-Luc Comolli and Paul Narboni in *Film Theory and Criticism*, edited by Leo Braudy and Marshall Cohen, Sixth Edition, Oxford University Press, 2004, p.813

7 Stanley Cavell, 'What Becomes of Things on Film' from *Themes Out Of School: Effects and Causes*, University of Chicago Press, 1988, pp.182–3.

8 Steve Neale, *Cinema and Technology: Image, Sound, Colour*, BFI Macmillan, 1985, p.50

9 Richard Dyer, *The Oxford Guide to Film Studies*, Oxford University Press, 1998, pp.4–5

10 Daniel Frampton, *Filmosophy*, Wallflower Press, London, 2006, p.6

11 Roland Barthes, quoted by Pam Cook and Mieke Bernink, *The Cinema Book*, BFI, 1999, p.33

12 Chris Barker, *Cultural Studies: Theory and Practice*, Sage, 2009, p.185

13 Richard Dyer, op cit, p.9

14 VF Perkins, *The Magnificent Ambersons*, BFI, 1999, p.18

15 Eugene Ionesco, taken from the Introduction to the stage play text *Rhinoceros*, Penguin Modern Classics, 1989

16 Samantha Long, *British Social Realism: From Documentary to Brit Grit*, Wallflower Press, 2008, p.5

17 André Bazin, *What Is Cinema?*, University of California Press, 2005, p.30

18 Ibid

19 EH Gombrich, *The Story of Art*, Phaidon, 2006, pp.390–1

20 Jean Renoir, *Senses of Cinema* website, www.sensesofcinema.com

21 Stanley Cavell, quoted in Pamela Robertson Wojcik, *Movie Acting: The Film Reader*, Routledge, 2004, p.20

22 Andre Bazin, 'The French Renoir' in *Jean Renoir*, WH Allen, New York, 1974, online at. http://wings.buffalo.edu/AandL/english/courses/eng201d/Renoir-Bazin.html

23 François Truffaut, letter to Jean Renoir, dated 13 November 1969 and published in *Jean Renoir: Letters*, David Thompson and Lorraine LoBianco (eds), Faber and Faber, 1994, p.496

24 Pam Cook and Mieke Bernink, op cit, p.51

25 Cameron Crowe, *Sight and Sound*, September 2002, p.32

26 Jean Renoir, *My Life in Film*, Da Capo Press, 1974, p.171

27 Akira Kurosawa quoted on DVD inlay for *The Satyajit Ray Collection*, Artifical Eye, 2008

28 DVD of the *Apu Trilogy*, BFI

29 Roger Ebert review of *La Règle du Jeu*, rogerebert.suntimes.com

30 Andrew Higson, 'Britain's Outstanding Contribution to the Film: The Documentary Realist Tradition' in Charles Barr (ed), *All Our Yesterdays*, BFI, 1990, p.74

31 Ken Loach, archive.sensesofcinema.com/contents/directors/03/loach.html

32 Samantha Long, op cit, p. 1

33 Roger Ebert review of *Kes*, rogerebert.suntimes.com

34 Derek Malcolm review of *Kes* in the *Guardian*, 22 June 2000, www.guardian.co.uk\

35 Peter Bondanella, *Italian Cinema: From Neorealism to the Present*, Continuum, 1994, p.32

36 Cesare Zavattini, quoted by Peter Bondanella, Ibid, p. 31

37 Ibid

38 François Truffaut, quoted by Philip Lopate in *Night and Fog* essay accompanying region 1 Criterion DVD of *Night and Fog*, www.criterion.com/current/posts/288-night-and-fog

39 Jean-Luc Godard quoted in Criterion essay about *Rome, Open City*, www.criterion.com

40   Janet Maslin, *The New York Times*, 9 January 1985

41   Thomas Elsaesser, *Metropolis*, BFI, 2000, p.7

42   Tom Charity, *The Rough Guide to Film*, Penguin, 2007, p.299

43   Hermann Warm in David Bordwell and Kristin Thompson (eds), *Film Art: An Introduction*, Seventh Edition, McGraw-Hill, 2003, p.472

44   Thomas Elsaesser, op cit, p.20

45   Review of *Metropolis* in *Der Tag* newspaper, referenced in Michael Minden and Holger Bachmann (eds), *Fritz Lang's Metropolis: Cinematic Visions of Technology and Fear*, Camden House, New York, 2000, p. 27

46   Martin Kroeber, quoted by David Bordwell in *Metropolis Unbound*, www.davidbordwell.net/blog/?p=7652

47   Tom Charity, op cit, p. 148

48   *Brightlights Film Journal*, www.brightlightsfilm.com/27/joanofarc.php

49   Paul Schrader, *Transcendental Style in Film*, Da Capo, 1988, p.122

50   Donald Skolker, *Dreyer in Double Reflection: Translation of Carl Th.Dreyer Writing About the Film*, Da Capo Press, 1973, quoted at www.senses ofcinema.com

51   Carl Th.Dreyer quoted by Roger Ebert, www.rogerebert.com.suntimes. com/apps/Feb16th1997

52   Ibid

53   Armond White, www.criterion.com, http://www.criterion.com/current/ posts/226-carl-th-dreyer

54   David Bordwell, 'The Art Cinema as a Mode of Film Practice' in *Film Theory and Criticism*, edited by Leo Braudy and Marshall Cohen, Oxford University Press, 2009, p.110

55   Ibid

56   David Bordwell, *Bergman, Antonioni and the Stubborn Stylists*, 11 August 2007, www.davidbordwell.net

57   Ingmar Bergman, quoted by Peter Cowie, *Ingmar Bergman: A Critical Biography*, Andre Deutsch, 1992, p.137

58   Ingmar Bergman, 'Pure Kamikaze', interview with Stig Bjorkman in *Sight and Sound* magazine, September 2002, p.16

59   David Bordwell, *Bergman, Antonioni and the Stubborn Stylists*, op cit

60   Norman McLaren, quoted in the booklet accompanying the DVD release *Norman McLaren: The Master's Collections*, Soda Pictures, 2007

61   Paul Wells, 'Animation: Forms and Meaning' in *An Introduction to Film Studies*, edited by Jill Nelmes, Second Edition, Routledge, 1999, p.238

62 Marcel Jean, *The Tireless Innovator*, National Film Board of Canada website, www3.nfb.ca/animation/objanim/en/filmmakers/Norman-McLaren/overview.php

63 Stan Brakhage, quoted by Liz Faber and Helen Walters, *Animation Unlimited: Innovative Short Film Since 1940*, Lawrence King, 2004, p.18

64 Stan Brakhage, 'Metaphors on Vision' in *Film Theory and Criticism*, op cit, p.199

65 Nicole Brenez and Adrian Martin, *Serious Mothlight For Stan Brakhage*, www.rouge.com.au/1/brakhage.html

66 Frédéric Back, speaking on *The Man Who Planted Trees* DVD, (region 1), CBC Radio Canada, 2004

67 Ibid

68 Frédéric Back discussing *The Mighty River*, www.fredericback.com

69 Paul Wells, *Understanding Animation*, Routledge, 1998, p.243

70 Kim Grant, *Surrealism and the Visual Arts*, Cambridge University Press, 2005, p.136

71 Phil Drummond, introduction to *Un Chien Andalou* screenplay, Faber and Faber, London, 1994, p.v

72 David Butler, *Fantasy Cinema: Impossible Worlds on Screen*, Wallflower Press, 2009, p.3

73 Jean Vigo, Foreword to *Un Chien Andalou* screenplay, op cit, p.xxv

74 Phil Drummond, introduction to *Un Chien Andalou* screenplay, Ibid, p.xxiii

75 Jean Cocteau, www.criterion.com/current/posts/250-once-upon-a-time-french-poet-explains-his-filming-of-fairy-tale

76 François Steegmuller, www.criterion.com/current/posts/17-beauty-and-the-beast

77 Ridley Scott discussing Jean Cocteau's *La Belle et la Bête* in the *Legend: Ultimate Edition* DVD Director's Commentary, Region 1, Universal, 2002

78 Andrew Moor, *Powell and Pressburger: A Cinema of Magic Spaces*, IB Tauris, 2005, p.223

79 Ian Christie, *Arrows of Desire: The Films of Michael Powell and Emeric Pressburger*, Faber and Faber, 1994, p.68

80 Ibid, p.69

81 Janet Leeper, *English Ballet*, Penguin Books, 1944, p.25

82 Ian Christie, www.criterion.com, http://www.criterion.com/current/posts/403-tales-from-the-lives-of-marionettes

83 *Monthly Film Bulletin*, Vol 18, No 209, June 1951, p. 277, www.screenonline.org

84 Jill Nelmes (ed), *An Introduction to Film Studies*, Routledge, Second Edition, 1999, p.214

85 Stella Bruzzi, *New Documentary: A Critical Introduction*, Routledge, 2000, p.68

86 Dziga Vertov, quoted by Jill Nelmes, *An Introduction to Film Studies*, op cit, p.191

87 David Bordwell and Kristin Thompson, *Film Art: An Introduction*, McGraw-Hill, 2003, p.130

88 Solinas and Gettino, 'Toward a Third Cinema' in *Movies and Methods*, Bill Nichols (ed), Vol 1, University of California Press, 1985, p.47

89 Bill Nichols, quoted by Thomas Austin, *Watching the World: Screen Documentary and Audience*, Manchester University Press, 2007, p.180

90 Godfrey Reggio, http://www.koyaanisqatsi.org/films/film.php

91 Ibid

92 Ian Aitken, 'The British Documentary Film Movement' in *The British Cinema*, Robert Murphy (ed), BFI, 2003, p.61

93 *Monthly Film Bulletin* review of *Night Mail*, www.screenonline.org.uk

94 Robert Flaherty, quoted by Roger Manville in *Cinema*, Penguin Books, London, 1950, reprinted in *Imagining Reality: The Faber Book of Documentary*, Mark Cousins and Kevin McDonald (eds), 1996, pp.37–8

95 Robert Flaherty, http://www.cinemaweb.com/silentfilm/bookshelf/23_rf1_2.htm

96 Roger Ebert, http://rogerebert.suntimes.com/apps/pbcs.dll/articleAID=/20050925/REVIEWS08/509250301/1023

97 Claude Lanzmann quoted by Stuart Liebermann in *Claude Lanzmann's Shoah: Key Essays*, Oxford University Press, 2007, p.49; book included with DVD set

98 Stella Bruzzi, *New Documentary: A Critical Introduction*, Routledge, 2000, p.105

99 Simone de Beauvoir, quoted by Stella Bruzzi, Ibid, p.106

100 Yoshifa Loshitzky, *Spielberg's Holocaust: Critical Perspectives on Schindler's List*, Indiana Univeristy Press, 1997, pp.104–5

101 Philip Groening, press notes for *Into Great Silence* (UK distributor Soda Pictures)

102 Ibid

103 *Guardian* review of *Into Great Silence*, 31 December 2006, www.guardian.co.uk/film/2006/dec/31/worldcinema.documentary

104 John Berger writing about Free Cinema, *Sight and Sound* online, http://www.bfi.org.uk/features/freecinema/archive/berger-lookatbritain.html

105 Dziga Vertov quoted in *The Rough Guide to Film*, Penguin Books, London, 2007, p.578

106 Vertov's manifesto, quoted by Graham Roberts in *The Man With the Movie Camera: The Film Companion*, IB Tauris, 2000, p.18

107 Graham Roberts, *The Man With the Movie Camera: The Film Companion*, Ibid, p.xiii

108 Paul Rotha, quoted by Graham Roberts, Ibid, p.99

109 Sergei Eisenstein, quoted by Jay Leda in *Kino: A History of Russian and Soviet Film*, Third Edition, Princeton University Press, 1983, p.194

110 David O Selznick quoted in article at http://archive.sensesofcinema.com/contents/cteq/00/4/potemkin.html

111 Andrew Higson, *Screen*, Vol 30, No 4, 1989, pp.36–7

112 Jean Luc-Godard quoted in *The Rough Guide to Film*, Penguin Books, London, 2007. No page number available.

113 Jill Forbes, 'The French New Wave' in *The Oxford Guide to Film Studies*, John Holls and Pamela Churchill (eds), Oxford University Press, 1998, p.461

114 Ibid, pp.464–5

115 Antoine de Basquet and Serge Toubiana, *Truffaut: A Biography*, University of California Press, 2000, p.175

116 Jean Renoir in a letter, 8 February 1962, letter archived at Films du Carosse

117 Whose review of *Jules et Jim* is this?

118 Peter Weir quoted in an interview with *Sight and Sound*, 1976, http://www.peterweircave.com/articles/articleg.html

119 Roger Ebert, http://rogerebert.suntimes.com/apps/pbcs.dll/article?AID=/19980802/REVIEWS08/401010325/1023

120 *Time Out* review of *Picnic At Hanging Rock*, http://www.timeout.com/film/reviews/71084/picnic-at-hanging-rock.html

121 Roger Cook and Gerd Germunden, *The Cinema of Wim Wenders: Image, Narrative and the Postmodern Condition*, Wayne State University Press, 1997, p.15

122 Ibid, p.12

123 Wim Wenders, *The Logic of Images: Essays and Conversations*, Faber and Faber, London, 1991, p.36

124 Ibid, pp.73–4

125 Roger Cook and Gerd Germunden, op cit, p.11

126 David Bordwell reviewing 'To the Distant Observer: Form and Meaning in the Japanese Cinema' by Noel Burch in *Wide Angle*, Vol 3, No 4, www.davidbordwell.net/articles/Bordwell_wide%20Angle_vol3_no4_70.pdf

127 Desson Howe, review of *Wings of Desire* in the *Washington Press*, 1 July 1988

128 Francis Ford Coppola, interview in *Little White Lies* magazine, No 29, May 2010

129 Douglas Pye, *The Movie Book of the Western*, Studio Vista, 1996, p.14

130 Jim Kitses, op cit, pp.21–2

131 Peter Fonda in conversation in a documentary about the making of *The Hired Hand*,, DVD, Tartan, 2004

132 Ibid

133 Vilmos Zsigmond in conversation in a documentary about the making of *The Hired Hand*, DVD, Tartan, 2004

134 Donald Richie, *A Hundred Years of Japanese Film*, Kodansha International, Tokyo, 2001 p.44

135 Ibid. p.54

136 Philip Kemp, *A Time of Honour: Seven Samurai and Sixteenth Century Japan*, www.criterion.com, http://www.criterion.com/current/posts/443-a-time-of-honor-seven-samurai-and-sixteenth-century-japan

137 Roger Ebert, http://rogerebert.suntimes.com/apps/pbcs.dll/article?AID=/20010819/REVIEWS08/401010356/1023

138 www.bfi.org.uk/features/kurosawa/book.html

139 Guillermo Del Toro, quoted by *Empire* magazine, Issue No 120, December 2006, p.109

140 Iñárritu, quoted by Chris Sullivan in 'Mexican Cinema: The New Aztec Camera' in the *Independent* newspaper, 8 September 2006

141 Guillermo Del Toro, quoted in 'Girl, Interrupted', *Sight and Sound* magazine, December 2006, http://www.bfi.org.uk/sightandsound/feature/49337/

142 Mark Kermode, *Sight and Sound*, December 2006, http://www.bfi.org.uk/sightandsound/feature/49337/

143 Guillermo Del Toro, quoted in 'Girl, Interrupted', op cit

144 www.empireonline.com review of *Pan's Labyrinth*, http://www.empireonline.com/reviews/reviewcomplete.asp?FID=134190

145 Peter Bradshaw, review of *Pan's Labyrinth*, http://www.guardian.co.uk/film/2006/nov/24/sciencefictionandfantasy.worldcinema

146 Review of *Pan's Labyrinth* in *Variety*, http://www.variety.com/index. asp?layout=print_review&reviewid=VE1117930674&categoryid=2471&q uery=pan%27s+labyrinth

147 Jean-Pierre Geuens, 'The Digital World Picture', *Film Quarterly*, No 55, p.21

148 Pam Cook and Mieke Bernink (eds) *The Cinema Book*, op cit, p.61

149 Patrick Keiller, quoted by Mark Fisher, 'English Pastoral', *Sight and Sound* magazine, November 2010, p.24

150 Ingmar Bergman, quoted in *Sight and Sound*, September 2002, p.15

151 Walter Murch discussing postproduction for the film *Tetro* at www.apple. com/pro/profiles/coppola_murch

152 *Atanarjuat: The Fast Runner* press kit

153 Sherril E Grace, *Canada and the Idea of North*, McGill-Queen's University Press, 2002. No page number available.

154 Jean-Pierre Geuens, 'The Digital World Picture', *Film Quarterly*, Vol 55, pp.16-27

155 Review of *Atanarjuat : The Fast Runner* from the *Village Voice* and located at www.isuma.tv/more-about-atanarjuat-fast-runner/atanarjuat-fast-runner-reviews

156 *Sight and Sound*, review of *Atanarjuat: The Fast Runner*, http://www.bfi. org.uk/sightandsound/feature/71/

157 Ibid

158 Richard Linklater, quoted in 'Animating a *Waking Life*', *Wired* magazine, 19 October 2001, http://www.wired.com/culture/lifestyle/news/2001/10/47433

159 Review of *Waking Life* in *Variety*, http://www.variety.com/review/ VE1117797159.html?categoryid=31&cs=1

160 Stanley Cavell, 'What Becomes of Thinking on Film' in *Themes Out of School: Effects and Causes*, University of Chicago Press, 1988, p.181

INDEX

www.kamerabooks.com

→ Comprehensive and up to date
   look at cult director Dario Argento

→ Accessible introduction to a
   general readership of Argento's
   work which will also appeal to
   hardcore fan base

Dario Argento
James Gracey

The stylistic and bloody excesses of the films of Dario Argento are instantly recognisable. Vivid, baroque and nightmarish, his films lock violent deaths in a twisted embrace with an almost sexual beauty.

Hailed as one of horror cinema's most significant pioneers and the twentieth century's major masters of the macabre, Argento continues to create inimitable and feverishly violent films with a level of artistry rarely seen in the horror genre, influencing the likes of Quentin Tarantino, John Carpenter and Martin Scorsese. His high profile is confirmed with his role as producer on celebrated classics such as George A. Romero's *Dawn of the Dead* and Lamberto Bava's *Demons*. This Kamera Book examines his entire output, including his most recent film *Giallo*.

978-1-84243-318-8   £12.99

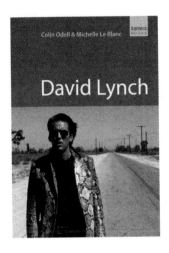

→ An in-depth look at America's most renowned film auteur, including biographical detail

→ Covers all his film and television work, including the latest mystery feature *INLAND EMPIRE*, as well as his non-film projects

→ Discusses key themes, styles and choice of stars

David Lynch

Colin Odell & Michelle Le Blanc

Internationally renowned, David Lynch is America's premier purveyor of the surreal, an artist whose work in cinema and television has exposed the world to his highly personalised view of society. This book examines his entire works, from the cult surrealism of his debut feature *Eraserhead* to his latest mystery, *INLAND EMPIRE*, considering the themes, motifs and stories behind his incredible films.

In Lynch's world the mundane and the fantastical collide, often with terrifying consequences. It is a place where the abnormal is normal, where the respectable becomes sinister, where innocence is lost and redemption gained at a terrible price. And there's always music in the air. David Lynch is your guide to this other world… and this is your guide to David Lynch.

978-1-84243-225-9   £9.99

→ **Considers Blaxploitation from the perspective of class and racial rebellion, genre – and Stickin' it to the Man**

→ **Over 60 blaxploitation films reviewed and discussed**

→ **Fully up to date, including *Baadassss* and *The Hebrew Hammer***

Blaxploitation Films
Mikel Koven

What is Blaxploitation? In the early 1970s a type of film emerged that featured all-black casts, really cool soul, R 'n' B and disco music soundtracks, characters sporting big guns, big dashikis, and even bigger 'fros, and had some of the meanest, baddest attitudes to shoot their way across our screens.

Blaxploitation Films considers Blaxploitation from the perspective of class and racial rebellion, genre – and Stickin' it to the Man, with over 60 Blaxploitation films reviewed and discussed. Sections include Blaxploitation horror films, kung-fu movies, Westerns and parodies and it is fully up to date, including *Baadassss* and *The Hebrew Hammer* and covers the deaths of Isaac Hayes and Rudy Rae Moore.

978-1-84243-334-8   £12.99